The Kitchen Goddess

More Vegetarian Recipes from the Shoshoni Yoga Retreat

Susannah Narayani Levine
artwork by Faith Stone

SGRY 2009
Prakasha Press

Published by SGRY
Prakasha Press
P.O. Box 400
Rollinsville, CO 80474-0400
USA

www.shoshoni.org
kailasa@shoshoni.org

ISBN 978-1-888386-15-8

Levine, Susannah Narayani
Kitchen Goddess: More Vegetarian Recipes from the Shoshoni Yoga Retreat
written by Susannah Narayani Levine
artwork by Faith Stone
1st edition

ISBN 978-1-888386-15-8

1. Vegetarian cookery. 2. Cookery, Yoga I. Levine, Susannah Narayani
II. Title

Printed in the United States

front cover: the lodge building and lake at Shoshoni Yoga Retreat in early autumn

This book is dedicated with love and devotion to
my teacher, Sri Shambhavananda,
and to Faith, who is also the mother of us all.

"White Tara" by Faith Stone

CONTENTS

Acknowledgements   vi

About the Author   vii

Introduction   ix

Glossary of Special Ingredients   xiv

Appetizers   20

Soups   30

Salads and Vegetable Side Dishes   46

Grains, Beans, and Noodles   62

Entrees   88

Bakery   114

Condiments, Dressings, and Accompaniments   132

Sweet Treats and Desserts   152

Menus   165

Index   168

Acknowledgements

I would like to thank Faith for her inspirational presence, both in the kitchen and out of it. Special thanks also to Ma Kripananda, for believing I could do it. Thanks to Kumara for volunteering so much time to design this cookbook. Many, many special thanks to all the wonderful cooks at Shoshoni, who helped inspire and test the recipes in this book. And thanks to our retreat guests who love eating here, and are always asking, "Where can I get this recipe?"

Susannah Narayani Levine
October 2009

About the Author

Susannah Narayani Levine has been a student of Sri Shambha-vananda since 2002. She has cooked thousands of meals for re-treat-goers at Shoshoni. Narayani has been playing in the kitchen since she could sit up. Her cooking teachers have been her mom and dad, chef Faith Stone, Shanti, and Kamala. Narayani has a Bachelor's degree in English and a Master's degree in Education. She also enjoys reading and playing the mandolin.

About the Artist

Faith Stone began her studies at the Museum of fine Arts in Boston while still in high school. She attended Montserrat School of visual arts in Beverly Massachusetts. She then pursued a career as a chef and owner of Rudi's Restaurant in Boulder, Colorado. Faith has published two cookbooks, *The Shoshoni Cookbook* and *The Yoga Kitchen*, and a novel, *Rudi and the Green Apple*.

Faith continued her visual arts studies with classes at CU Boulder and studied Thangka painting for three years at Naropa University. Faith's paintings are held in private collections in the US and India. Faith taught middle and high school art at Hualalai Academy in Kailua-Kona, Hawaii. She currently is an award winning high school art teacher in Boulder, Colorado and exhibits in group shows at the Boulder Museum of Contemporary Art (Voices 3), Rembrandt Gallery (Voices 4), Colorado Art Educators annual juried show, and solo exhibits at Shoshoni Yoga Retreat and Eldorado Yoga Ashram. Faith is the director of Eldorado Yoga summer camp. She loves teaching art and working with kids!

Introduction

About Shoshoni

"Shoshoni is the mother of us all," our teacher, Sri Shambhavananda, once said. He meant that Shoshoni is a place where people come to be nourished on many levels. The yoga retreat center and residential ashram is a place where thousands of guests come each year to stay and take yoga classes, chant, meditate, and of course, eat wonderful vegetarian food. Some also come to the ashram to devote a month, six months, or a year to expanding their spiritual life.

Shoshoni's sweet atmosphere is like an umbrella, offering cool sweetness to those who visit, whether for a day, a week, or longer. Eating our nourishing food is a big part of that experience for many who come here.

About Our Teacher

Rishi Mahamandaleshwar Sri Shambhavananda, affectionately known as Babaji, is the founder of Shoshoni and the Shambhava School of Yoga. A warm-hearted, loving spiritual teacher, he has created numerous centers across the country where people can go to learn about yoga, meditation, and living a spiritual life. It is his vision that brought Shoshoni to life, and which sustains the incredible level of energy that permeates the retreat center. He teaches simple meditation practices with the power to transform lives.

About the Divine Mother

We all have a little bit of the Goddess in us. Whether we are a man or a woman, old or young, and no matter where we were born, we all came into the world through a mother. When we eat and nourish our body, mind, and spirit through wonderful food, we are honoring our mothers.

Mothers come in many forms. They can be birth mothers, adopted mothers, wives, sisters, aunts, and good friends. A mother is a powerful role model, guide, and helper. The Divine Mother, the feminine aspect of God, is all of these things. She is the shakti, or manifest spiritual energy that lives in all people.

In Eastern traditions, such as Hinduism and Tibetan Buddhism, there are many different goddesses. Saraswati, the wisdom goddess, rides on a beautiful swan and dresses in white. She plays the vina, an Indian stringed instrument. Gentle and kind, she presides over higher learning, music, and the arts. Lakshmi, the nourishment goddess, sits on a huge lotus flower. She holds two lotus flowers in her hands and bestows blessings through a shower of gold coins flowing out of her palms. Durga, the transformation goddess, rides on a fierce lion. She has ten arms, which hold a variety of weapons for destroying our difficulties. Strong and protective, she can remove many obstacles in life. Kali, the dark goddess, has black skin and wears a necklace of skulls. Intense and powerful, she helps us face our inner demons, and she removes all darkness. Tara is a female emanation of the Buddha. She represents compassion and wisdom.

The Ma Shrine

Visitors to Shoshoni always love the Ma Shrine, a beautiful sacred space devoted to the Divine Mother. Inside the shrine is beautiful artwork depicting the goddesses, thangka paintings, statues, and fragrant flowers. Guests can sit in the rocking chair, meditate, and soak in the beautiful energy of the Mas. Sitting in the Ma Shrine feels like getting a great big hug from your mom!

The artwork in this book was inspired by the goddesses in the Ma Shrine at Shoshoni and in the Dome at our Eldorado Springs ashram.

Cooking with Shakti

The art of cooking with shakti is as simple as cooking with love. I will never forget the first time I visited my husband's grandmother. She cooked us a simple Italian dinner. When I took the first bite, I felt so much love in the food that every bite was pure nourishment for the spirit. That's why your mom's cooking always tastes best: because she loves you!

People often remark that Shoshoni food tastes like a home-cooked meal, only better. They want to know what we put in all this wonderful food. Of course, we start with organic, fresh, whole foods, but the secret ingredient is love.

In the Shoshoni kitchen, the cooks focus on repeating mantra and chanting as they cook. Saying mantra helps us focus on the state of love and happiness that exists inside of us. As we focus on that place, we put some of that happiness into the food, too!

Blessing the Food

At Shoshoni, as we prepare to cook, we light a bit of incense, ring a bell, or light a candle. We have set up a little altar in our kitchen with pictures of deities and loved ones. We think of the people we are going to be cooking for with love. We think of the Inner Self, the divine spark that exists inside all of us, with love.

As we cook, we allow ourselves to stay in that state of sweetness and giving. We don't argue in the kitchen, or think negative thoughts about the food or ourselves. We say mantra while we cook, and bring our full attention to each action in the kitchen. We allow our kitchen to become a sacred space, a place we can go to relax and connect to the flow of shakti, or spiritual energy, that nourishes everyone.

We also offer a little bit of the food we cook at our altar. When we offer the food before eating it, then our entire meal becomes prasad, a blessed offering.

Mantras to Use in the Kitchen

Om Gam Ganapataye Namah
I bow with respect to Ganesha, the Remover of Obstacles.

Om Namah Shivaya
I bow with respect to my Inner Self.

Om Aim Hrim Klim Chamundaye Vicce
I bow with respect to the Goddess, in Her many forms.

Om Annapurne Sada Purne
Shankara Prana Vallabhe
Jnana Vairagya Siddhyartham
Bhiksham Dehi Namostute
I bow with respect to the Goddess, who is full, complete, and perfect
with food and grains.

Om Krim Kalyai Namah
I bow with respect to Kali, the Remover of Darkness.

Om Hrim Shrim Dum Durgyai Namah
I bow with respect to Durga, the Remover of Difficulties.

Om Shrim Lakshmyai Namah
I bow with respect to Lakshmi, the Bestower of Abundance.

Om Aim Saraswatyai Namah
I bow with respect to Saraswati, the Goddess of Arts and Speech.

Glossary of Specialty Ingredients

These are some of the specialty ingredients we often use in the Shoshoni kitchen. Most are readily available at your grocery store or health food store. You might find a few of them in Asian or Indian grocery stores or other specialty foods markets in your area.

Asafetida or hing: Asafetida is a commonly used Ayurvedic spice. It is a resin from the asafetida plant. Commonly called hing, asafetida has a flavor similar to garlic. Asafetida can be found in the bulk spice section of your natural food store or at an Indian market.

Basmati rice: Basmati rice is a long-grain Indian rice with a delicate fragrance. It can be found in most grocery stores. Whenever possible, this rice is the preferred variety to serve with Indian food!

Black sesame seed: Black sesame seeds can be found at most natural foods stores or Indian markets. They are the same size as white sesame seeds, but dark in color. They have a mild, nutty flavor.

Filo dough: Filo dough is a thin pastry dough that comes in Middle Eastern recipes. Filo is available in the frozen foods section of most grocery stores.

Idli mix: Idli mix is usually available at Indian foods stores. It is made of rice flour, dal flour, and leavening. Using the mix is easier than making your own, but you can buy these specialty flours separately, too.

Jasmine rice: Jasmine rice is a fragrant long-grain rice with a floral aroma. It comes in brown and white varieties. Jasmine rice is available at most grocery stores and natural foods stores.

Jicama: Jicama is a root vegetable from Mexico. On the outside, it looks like a huge turnip. Inside, it is crunchy, juicy, and white. Often served raw, it is great as a salad or slaw addition. Jicama is available in most grocery stores in the summer.

Kasha: Kasha is toasted buckwheat groats. Nutty in flavor and high in protein, it is a staple Eastern European grain. You can often find it in the bulk section of natural foods stores, or the Jewish food section of grocery stores.

Mascarpone: This mild Italian fresh cheese is like a cross between ricotta and cream cheese. It can be found in the specialty cheese section of most grocery stores.

Masa harina: Masa harina is finely ground corn flour. It is used to make tamales and other South and Central American delicacies. You can find it in Mexican groceries and in the Mexican foods section of your grocery store.

Matzo meal: Matzo meal is finely ground matzo crackers. It is available in the Jewish food section of the grocery store.

Mung dal: Dal refers to a split pea or bean soup, or the split peas or beans used as a main ingredient in the soup. Mung dal can be made with whole green mung beans, split mung beans with the skins on, or split mung beans with the skins removed. The latter is referred to as "golden mung dal." These varieties can be found in Indian and Asian foods stores.

Nutritional yeast: A popular vegetarian food supplement, nutritional yeast contains high concentrations of B vitamins and protein. It is available in powder or flake form at natural foods stores.

Panir: This quick and easy homemade cheese makes any curry dish special. It is made by boiling whole milk and separating it into curds and whey with the addition of lime juice or a little vinegar. The curds are then strained through a cheese cloth and allowed to harden into a simple cheese. Cut the cheese into pieces and pan-fry it until it is browned. Panir adds flavor and protein to a meal.

Pickled ginger: Pickled ginger is available in a jar at most Asian foods stores. It can be pink in color, or white.

Rice noodles: Rice noodles are available in many shapes and varieties. For the purposes of Asian cooking, select the translucent variety, which comes in thin and wide widths. You can also purchase rice spaghetti, which is not translucent, and which looks a lot like regular spaghetti when cooked. This can be substituted for regular pasta in Italian meals, if you have a sensitivity to wheat.

Silken tofu: Silken tofu is available in the refrigerator or produce section of many grocery stores. It has a smooth, silky texture which makes it perfect for blending into desserts. If you are using tofu in a stir fry or main dish, however, choose regular tofu instead of silken tofu.

Soba Noodles: Soba noodles are long, thin noodles made from buckwheat. They can be found in the Asian section of most grocery stores.

Soy "Sausage": Many different brands of meatless soy products are available in the grocery store, usually in the frozen foods section. They make an interesting change of pace when added to traditional vegetarian fare. Try a recipe with soy "sausage" for a different experience in vegetarian food! Meatless products add protein and vitamins to your meal.

Sucanat: Sucanat is a trademark name for evaporated cane juice crystals combined with blackstrap molasses. We use it as one of our main sweeteners because it has more to offer us nutritionally than other sweeteners. Sucanat will impart a rich flavor and deep, dark color to your pasteries. If you want a lighter result, use granulated fructose or natural cane sugar.

Tahini: Tahini is pureed sesame seeds. It is creamy, nutty, and slightly bitter in taste. It also thickens sauces when blended in and cooked. You can find it at most grocery stores in the nut butter section.

Tomatillos: Tomatillos look like small green tomatoes. They are a staple of Mexican and Central American food. Try adding them to recipes that call for tomatoes. They are available in the summertime in most grocery stores.

TVP: TVP is textured vegetable protein, a soy-based product. It comes in large chunks or small pieces. When you buy it (usually in bulk at the natural foods store), it is dry. Soak it in warm water before beginning to cook with it. It soaks up the flavor of whatever you are cooking, and adds a lot of protein with virtually no fat!

"Radha Krishna"by Faith Stone

"The heart is the hub of all holy places.
Go there and roam in it."

Appetizers

Bruschetta   21

Sweet Potato Koftas   22

Vegetable Bhajis   23

Stuffed Portabella Mushrooms   24

Tofu Meatballs   25

Asparagus Filo Spring Rolls   26

Cream Cheese Wontons   27

Chinese Dumplings with Cabbage and Star Anise   28

Bruschetta

This classic appetizer is simplicity itself, and very, very delicious. Substitute soy cheese for the cheese if you prefer.

1 whole grain French baguette

2 T. olive oil

6 Roma tomatoes, diced

10 basil leaves

2 t. Balsamic vinegar

1/2 t. salt

1/4 t. black pepper

1/2 c. shredded mozzarella cheese

1. Preheat the oven to 450. Place one rack on the top of the oven.

2. Slice the baguette into 1-inch thick slices. Brush both sides of the pieces with olive oil and arrange on a cookie sheet. Brown the bread in the oven for 5-7 minutes, until crisp but not hard.

3. Combine the diced tomatoes, Balsamic vinegar, salt and pepper. Thinly slice the basil leaves and stir to combine them with the tomato mixture.

4. Spread the tomato mixture on the toasted bread, and top with a sprinkle of mozzarella cheese. Place the bruschetta on the top rack of the oven for 8-10 minutes, until the cheese is melted and slightly browned. Serve immediately.

Sweet Potato Koftas

Serves 4-6

Koftas can be made from many combinations of shredded vegetables. These are earthy and sweet, with a beautiful orange color. Try serving them with Raita, p. 142.

4 medium sweet potatoes, peeled

1/2 medium onion, peeled

3/4 c. unbleached all-purpose flour

1 t. curry powder

1 t. cumin

1/2 t. tumeric

1/2 t. coriander

1/2 t. salt

1/2 t. baking powder

1/2 c. canola oil

1. Using a food processor or a hand grater, shred the sweet potatoes and the onion.

2. In a separate bowl, combine the flour, curry powder, cumin, tumeric, coriander, salt, and baking powder. Stir the dry ingredients into the shredded vegetables, and stir to coat.

3. Heat the canola oil on medium heat in the bottom of a small cast-iron skillet. Form one-inch balls out of the vegetable mixture, and drop them into the oil. Fry the koftas for about 5 minutes on each side, turning until they are browned evenly all over.

4. Place the koftas on a paper towel to cool. Serve immediately with yogurt raita as a dipping sauce.

Vegetable Bhajis

Serves 4-6

These vegetable fritters are a delicious addition to any Indian feast! You can make them ahead of time and warm them in the oven for serving later, but they are best right out of the pan. You can serve them with any chutney, like Pear-Mint Chutney, p. 144.

1 c. unbleached enriched flour

1 T. baking powder

1 t. salt

1/2 t. cumin, ground

1/2 t. tumeric

1/2 t. coriander

1/4 t. asafetida

1/2 c. cauliflower, thinly sliced

1/2 c. cabbage, thinly sliced

1/4 c. onion, thinly sliced

3/4 c. cold water

oil for frying

1. In a medium bowl, whisk together the unbleached flour, baking powder, salt, cumin, tumeric, coriander, and asafetida. Add the cauliflower, cabbage, and onion, and stir to coat with the flour mixture.

2. Drizzle the water over the flour mixture and stir until just combined. The mixture will be lumpy.

3. In a medium cast-iron skillet, heat 2 inches of oil over medium high heat. Drop tablespoons of the pakora mixture into the oil and fry for 1-2 minutes on each side, until golden brown. Remove with a slotted spoon and let cool on paper towels. Serve hot.

Stuffed Portabella Mushrooms

Serves 4

This appetizer doubles as a simple meal! Serve alone, with bread, or as an accompaniment to pasta, rice, or other grain pilafs.

4 portabella mushrooms, stems removed and chopped

1 T. olive oil

1/2 medium onion

1 stalk celery, diced

1 clove garlic, minced

1/4 c. bread crumbs

1/4 c. walnuts, finely chopped

1/4 c. goat cheese, feta cheese, or Tofu Feta, p. 145

1/2 t. salt

1/4 t. pepper

1. Preheat the oven to 400. Wash the mushrooms and dry them with a paper towel. Finely chop the mushroom stems.

2. In a skillet, heat the olive oil over medium heat. Sauté the onion, garlic, and celery until soft. Add the chopped mushroom stems and continue cooking for another 1-2 minutes. Remove the mixture into a small mixing bowl. Add the bread crumbs, walnuts, and cheese. Stir, and add the salt and pepper.

3. Heat the same skillet to medium heat. Place the whole mushroom tops in the pan. Cook the mushroom tops for 3-4 minutes on each side, until they begin to brown.

4. Place the mushroom tops on a baking sheet, and fill each top with a spoonful of the filling mixture. Bake the mushrooms in the oven for 15 minutes, until the cheese is melted and the mushrooms are cooked through. Serve hot.

The Kitchen Goddess

Tofu Meatballs

Serves 6-8

These "meatballs" are delicious with any kind of pasta, or just served with marinara sauce for dipping as an appetizer. Try them with Carrot Marinara, p. 110.

1 lb. firm tofu

1/2 c. walnuts

3 T. whole wheat pastry flour

3 T. soy sauce

1 t. sage, dried

1 t. basil

1/2 t. rosemary

1 t. salt

1/4 t. black pepper

1. Preheat the oven to 375. Oil a baking sheet.

2. In the food processor, grind the walnuts to a fine powder. Remove the walnuts and place them in a medium mixing bowl.

3. Place half of the tofu in the food processor and process to a smooth paste. Add to the mixing bowl.

4. Crumble the remaining tofu with your fingers and place in the mixing bowl. Add the flour, soy sauce, sage, basil, rosemary, salt, and pepper. Mix until all ingredients are combined.

5. Roll the mixture into 1-inch balls and place on the cookie sheet. Bake 25-30 minutes, until the meatballs look medium brown on the outside, and feel springy to the touch (not soft).

6. Remove from the oven and let cool. Serve with pasta and marinara sauce.

Asparagus Filo Spring Rolls

Serves 4-6

Elegant and easy, filo dough is a crowd pleaser! You can make these rolls ahead of time, and then bake them right before serving. They are best right out of the oven.

1 package of filo dough

1/4 c. olive oil

10 asparagus stalks

1 red bell pepper, sliced

2 carrots, peeled

2 zucchinis

1 clove garlic, minced

1/2 t. rosemary

1/2 t. thyme

1/2 t. salt

1/4 t. black pepper

1. Preheat the oven to 400. Snap the asparagus stalks off near the bottom of the stalk; where the asparagus breaks naturally is where the tender part of the vegetable ends. Slice the carrots and zucchini into long, thin pieces about 1/2 inch thick.

2. Heat 1 T. of the olive oil in a skillet over medium heat. Sauté the bell pepper, carrot, and garlic for about 5 minutes, until tender. Add the zucchini and asparagus and cook for 2 minutes longer. Add the rosemary, thyme, salt and pepper, and remove from the heat.

3. On a clean work surface, spread out one sheet of filo dough. Brush the dough with olive oil. Lay another sheet of filo on top and brush with olive oil. Repeat until you have used 4 sheets of filo dough.

4. For each roll, use about an eighth of the vegetable mixture. Lay the vegetables lengthwise along the filo. Fold the sides in and roll the filo up into a cylinder. Place the roll on an oiled cookie sheet, and brush the top with olive oil. Repeat with the other vegetables.

5. Bake the rolls in the oven for 15-20 minutes, until golden brown. Serve immediately.

The Kitchen Goddess

Cream Cheese Wontons

Serves 4-6

This vegetarian version of a classic Chinese appetizer is always a hit at Shoshoni dinners. Try them with Sweet and Sour Sauce, p. 140.

1 package egg roll wrappers

8 oz. cream cheese

1/4 c. minced onion

2 T. warm water

1/2 t. red chili flakes

1/4 t. salt

Canola oil for frying

1. Cut the egg roll wrappers into quarters, making four squares out of each.

2. In a bowl, soak the red chili flakes in the warm water for 10 minutes. Drain the water and set aside.

3. In a food processor, whip the cream cheese for 1-2 minutes, until smooth. Add the minced onion, chili flakes, and salt, and process to combine.

4. Place one teaspoon of the cream cheese mixture in the center of a wonton wrapper. Moisten the edges of the square with water, and fold the corners of the square to the center. Press the edges of the wrapper together, creating a pyramid shape. Set the wonton on a cookie sheet and repeat until you have used the rest of the filling.

5. Heat the 2-3 inches of canola oil in a cast iron skillet to medium heat. Drop 2-3 wontons in the oil at a time, frying them for 1-2 minutes, until golden brown. Remove with a slotted spoon and drain on a paper towel. Serve immediately.

Chinese Dumplings with Cabbage and Star Anise

Serves 4-6

Steamed dumplings are warming and grounding in the fall and winter season. This recipe uses green cabbage, but you can add shredded carrots or bok choy, too.

1 package egg roll wrappers

1 medium onion, sliced

4 c. green cabbage, shredded

2 T. dark sesame oil

1 T. fresh ginger, minced

1/2 t. salt

1/8 t. star anise powder

1/4 t. white pepper

1/2 c. vegetable broth or water

1. In a medium skillet, heat one tablespoon of the sesame oil over medium high heat. Sauté the onion in the oil for about 5 minutes, until it begins to look translucent. Add the ginger, salt, star anise, and white pepper and stir.

Add the cabbage and cover the pan with a lid. Steam on medium heat for 1-2 minutes, until the cabbage is softened.

2. Place 2 tablespoons of the cabbage filling in the center of an egg roll wrapper. Moisten the edges with water and fold the corners towards the center, pinching the top into a purse shape. Repeat with the other wrappers.

3. Heat another skillet to medium heat. Coat the bottom of the pan with the second half of the sesame oil. Place the dumplings, pinched edges down, into the pan. Pour the vegetable broth or water over the top, cover, and steam the dumplings for 2-3 minutes.

4. Remove from the pan and serve hot or at room temperature.

"Shiva and Parvati" by Faith Stone

"All your joys are inside you in their fullness."
— **Bhagavan Nityananda**

Soups

Matzo Ball Soup   31

Curry Apple Squash   32

Tamale Soup   33

Mediterranean Creamy Tomato   34

Lima Bean and Soy "Sausage" Soup   35

Grilled Corn Chowder with Chipotle Peppers   36

Creamy Carrot Ginger   37

Sundried Tomato Chili with Textured Soy Protein   38

Idli Sambar   39

Mulligatawny   40

Lakshman's Butternut Squash and Coconut Kitchari   41

Ethiopian Lentil Stew - Yemesir Wat   42

Thai Coconut-Ginger Soup   43

Matzo Ball Soup

An all-time favorite soup at Shoshoni. Matzo balls have a comforting, homey appeal, and bring back childhood memories of Mom's kitchen!

1 t. canola oil

1 medium onion, diced

1 1/2 cloves garlic, minced

3 stalks celery, minced

2 medium carrots, minced

1/2 t. thyme

1/4 t. celery seed

2 T. nutritional yeast

2 T. soy sauce

2 t. salt

10 c. water or vegetable broth

2 eggs

2 T. canola oil

2 T. water or seltzer water

1/2 c. matzo meal

1/2 t. salt

1/2 t. black pepper

1. In a large saucepan, heat the canola oil over medium heat. Sauté the onion for 5 minutes, until translucent.

2. Add the garlic, celery, carrot, thyme, and celery seed. Sauté for 5 minutes, until the vegetables are tender. Add the water or broth, nutritional yeast, soy sauce, and salt. Cover, and bring the soup to a boil. Lower the heat and simmer on low for 20 minutes.

3. In a small mixing bowl, beat the eggs, oil, and water together until smooth. Stir in the matzo meal and salt until just combined. Cover and place the mixture in the refrigerator for 20 minutes.

4. Roll golf-ball sized balls of the matzo mixture with your hands, and drop into the boiling soup. Cover, and simmer on low for 30 minutes. Taste the soup and add salt to taste. Add the black pepper at the end.

5. Serve one matzo ball per bowl, and ladle the broth on top.

Curry Apple Squash Soup

Serves 6-8

This soup is simple to make, and absolutely delicious. The unusual combination of ingredients blend together perfectly. The oatmeal makes the soup creamy and silky with no added dairy.

1 t. canola oil

1 medium onion, diced

1 medium butternut squash, peeled and cubed

2 medium green apples, peeled and cubed

1 T. curry powder

1/2 t. garlic powder

1/4 c. dry oatmeal

6 c. water or vegetable broth

4 t. salt

2 T. lemon juice

1/4 c. plain yogurt

1. In a large saucepan, heat the canola oil over medium heat. Sauté the onion for 5 minutes, until translucent.

2. Add the squash, apples, curry powder, garlic powder, oatmeal and water. Cover the pot and simmer on medium-low until the squash and apples are very soft, about 45 minutes.

3. Blend the soup in the blender in 2-3 batches, processing it until it is smooth and creamy. Return the soup to the pot, add the salt and lemon juice, and heat through.

4. Serve hot with a dollop of yogurt on top.

The Kitchen Goddess

Tamale Soup

My mom used to make this soup, a spicy tomato bisque with Mexican flavors. The corn meal helps thicken the soup, and adds a texture reminiscent of a tamale.

1 T. corn oil or canola oil

1 medium onion, diced

2 cloves garlic, minced

2 stalks celery, diced

6 medium Roma tomatoes, diced

1/2 c. tomato paste

1 T. mild chili powder

1 t. oregano

1/2 t. dried sage powder

1/8 t. cayenne pepper

8 c. water or vegetable broth

1/4 c. corn meal

1 c. milk or plain soymilk

2 t. salt

1. In a large saucepan, heat the oil over medium heat. Sauté the onion for 5 minutes, until translucent. Add the garlic and celery and sauté for 2-3 minutes more.

2. Stir in the diced tomatoes, tomato paste, chili powder, oregano, sage, and cayenne. Sauté for 2-3 minutes, until the tomatoes are soft. Stir in the tomato paste, coating the vegetables. Add the water or broth and whisk to blend the mixture. Cover and heat on medium until the mixture boils. Lower the heat and simmer for 20 minutes.

3. Blend the soup in the blender in batches until smooth, and then return it to the pot. Heat until just boiling, then stir in the cornmeal. Simmer the soup on low for 15 minutes, until the cornmeal is soft, not gritty.

4. Stir in the milk or soymilk and add the salt. Serve hot, with shredded cheddar cheese or scallions on top.

Mediterranean Creamy Tomato Soup

Serves 3-4

Growing up, I lived near a lot of locally-owned Lebanese cafes. Every one of them offered this soup on the menu. The large amount of basil gives it a sweet, garden fresh flavor.

1/4 c. ghee or canola oil

1 medium onion, diced

2 cloves garlic, minced

2 stalks celery, minced

1/4 t. celery seed

2 c. diced tomatoes

1/3 c. tomato paste

1/4 c. unbleached all purpose flour

5 c. water or vegetable broth

2 c. milk or plain soymilk

1 t. salt

1/4 c. fresh basil, chopped

1. In a large saucepan, heat the ghee or oil over medium heat. Add the onion, and sauté until translucent. Add the garlic, celery, and celery seed, and sauté for 5 minutes more.

2. Add the diced tomatoes, and sauté for 2-3 minutes. Add the tomato paste and stir to coat the vegetables. Add the flour and stir until the mixture is just combined.

3. Whisking as you pour, add the water or broth a cup at a time. Cover and heat on medium until the soup begins to boil. Remove from the heat

4. Blend the soup in batches in the blender until smooth, then return it to the soup pot. Add the milk or soymilk and salt, and heat until just under boiling. Sprinkle the basil on top before serving. Serve hot.

The Kitchen Goddess

Lima Bean and Soy "Sausage" Soup

Serves 4-6

In the fall, we all wish for a hearty, warming soup. This one fits the bill perfectly. A meal in itself with a loaf of fresh bread, it can also be prepared in a Crockpot while you are away.

1 t. olive oil

1 medium onion, diced

2 cloves garlic, minced

1 stalk celery, diced

1 medium carrot, diced

1 medium tomato, diced

1/2 c. green pepper, diced

1/2 c. red pepper diced

4 c. cooked lima beans, fresh or frozen

1/2 t. thyme

1/2 t. rosemary

1/2 t. sage

1/2 t. basil

8 c. water or vegetable broth

1/4 c. soy sauce

1 t. canola oil

12 oz. soy "sausage"

1/2 t. salt

1/2 t. black pepper

1. In a large saucepan, heat the olive oil over medium heat. Sauté the onions for 5 minutes, until translucent. Add the garlic, celery, carrot, tomato, green pepper, and red pepper. Sauté for 5-7 minutes, until the vegetables begin to soften. Add the lima beans, thyme, rosemary, sage, basil, water, and soy sauce.

2. Bring the soup to a boil over medium high heat, then reduce the heat to low, cover, and simmer for 30 minutes.

3. In a separate skillet, heat the canola oil over medium high heat. Crumble the soy "sausage" into the pan and sauté for 5 minutes, or until lightly browned. Add the salt and pepper.

4. Stir the sausage into the soup immediately before serving. Add salt to taste.

Grilled Corn Chowder with Chipotle Peppers

Serves 4-6

I love simple soups, ones that only use a few ingredients, but use them to their best advantage! This soup tastes like summer to me. Grilling the corn adds a toasty, golden flavor to the soup.

1 T. olive oil

1 medium onion, diced

2 cloves garlic, minced

1 T. cumin seed

4 c. corn kernels

2 tomatillos, diced (use tomatoes if unavailable)

1 fresh or dried chipotle pepper, minced

6 c. water or vegetable broth

2 t. salt

1/2 t. black pepper

1. Heat a large cast-iron skillet or griddle to high heat. Add the olive oil, onion and garlic, and sauté for 2-3 minutes. Add the corn and cumin and grill over high heat until the corn is golden brown on the outside.

2. Stir in the tomatillos and chipotle pepper and sauté for 2-3 more minutes.

3. In a blender, puree half of the corn mixture and the water on high speed for 3-4 minutes, until completely smooth. Pour into a medium pot, and add the remaining corn to the soup. Add the salt and pepper. Heat until boiling and serve hot.

Creamy Carrot-Ginger Soup

Serves 4-6

Another Shoshoni classic. This soup is spicy and grounding in the fall and winter, and the beautiful orange color makes it very visually striking.

1 T. olive oil

1 medium onion, diced

2 T. fresh ginger, minced

1 clove garlic, minced

1/2 t. thyme

1/2 t. rosemary

1 bay leaf

6 large or 9 medium carrots, peeled and chopped

8 c. water or vegetable broth

1 c. milk or plain soymilk

1 t. salt

1/2 t. white pepper

1. In a large saucepan, heat the oil over medium heat. Sauté the onion for 5 minutes, until translucent. Add the ginger, garlic, thyme, rosemary, and bay leaf, and sauté for 2-3 minutes longer. Add the carrots and water, cover, and heat until boiling. Reduce the heat to low, and simmer for 30 minutes, until the carrots are very soft.

2. In a blender, puree the soup in batches for 2-3 minutes until very smooth. Return the soup to the soup pot. Stir in the milk, salt, and pepper, and heat through. Serve hot.

Sundried Tomato Chili with Textured Soy Protein

Serves 4-6

This vegetarian version of a classic soup uses TVP, textured vegetable protein. A versatile substance made from soy, TVP has a chewy, satisfying texture. You can buy it in bulk in most health food stores.

1 T. corn oil or olive oil

1 medium onion, diced

2 cloves garlic, minced

2 stalks celery, diced

1 green pepper, diced

2 tomatoes, diced

1 c. cooked pinto beans

2 T. chili powder

2 t. lemon juice

1 t. Tabasco sauce

1/2 t. oregano

1/2 t. sage

8 c. water or vegetable broth

1/2 c. sundried tomatoes

1 c. dry textured vegetable protein (TVP) granules

1 T. canola oil

2 c. boiling water

1 t. salt

1. In a large saucepan, heat the corn oil over medium heat. Sauté the onion for 5 minutes, until translucent. Add the garlic, celery, green pepper, tomatoes, and pinto beans. Sauté for 5 more minutes. Stir in the chili powder, lemon juice, Tabasco, oregano, and sage. Add the water or broth to the vegetables and bring the mixture to a boil. Cover, lower the heat to low, and simmer for 15 minutes.

2. In a small bowl, soak the sundried tomatoes in 1 cup of the boiling soup. Let the tomatoes soak for 15 minutes. In a blender, blend the soaked tomatoes and water and add to the chili.

3. In another bowl, pour 1 cup of boiling water over the TVP granules. Let the TVP soak for 10 minutes.

4. In a skillet, heat the canola oil over medium heat. Sauté the TVP for 3-5 minutes, until golden brown. Add to the chili. Add the salt, cover, and simmer on low heat for 30 more minutes. Serve hot.

The Kitchen Goddess

Idli Sambar

This classic Indian dish consists of a small rice dumpling, the idli, covered in a spicy lentil soup. It can be served as a main dish with a side of Naan bread, p. 120. To make the idlis, you will need to find idli mix, a rice flour mixture available in most Indian grocery stores. These stores usually carry idli steamers as well. An idli steamer looks like a regular stainless steel steam basket, but has 4 divets for holding the idli batter as it steams.

1 package idli mix

1 T. canola oil

1 medium onion, diced

1 t. red chili flakes

1/2 t. garlic

1/2 t. curry powder

1/2 t. fennel seeds

1/2 t. cumin, ground

2 c. red lentils

8 c. water

1 t. salt

1 t. fresh lemon juice

1/2 t. ground coriander

1. In a large saucepan, heat the canola oil over medium heat. Sauté the onion, red chili flakes, and garlic for 5 minutes. Add the curry powder, fennel seeds, and cumin, and sauté for 2-3 more minutes. Stir in the red lentils, coating them with the spices.

2. Add the water to the pot, cover, and bring to a boil. Reduce the heat and simmer on low for 30-40 minutes, until the lentils are very soft and almost dissolving.

3. Prepare the idli mixture according to package directions; usually this involves simply adding water to the rice flour mixture. In a large saucepan, bring 1 inch of water to a boil. Oil a set of idli steamers, and place 2 tablespoons of idli batter in each pocket. Place the steamer over the boiling water, cover the pot, and steam for 20 minutes. Remove the idlis from the steamer with a rubber spatula.

4. Stir the salt, lemon juice, and coriander into the lentil sambar. Heat through.

5. Place 2 idlis in each bowl and ladle the sambar on top. Serve immediately.

Mulligatawny Soup

Serves 4-6

This curry soup combines Continental and Indian flavors. It has all the comfort of vegetable soup with a spicy curry kick. It is beautiful as well as delicious; be extravagant and creative with the garnishes!

1 T. ghee or olive oil

1 medium onion, diced

2 cloves garlic, minced

2 stalks celery, diced

2 carrots, peeled and diced

1 red pepper, diced

1 sweet potato, peeled and diced

1/2 c. corn kernels

1 T. curry powder

1 T. fresh lemon juice

1 t. cumin, ground

1/4 t. tumeric

8 c. water or vegetable broth

1 c. cooked lentils

1/2 c. raw cashews

1 c. coconut milk

1 t. salt

Garnishes:
plain yogurt, chopped green apples, toasted coconut, currants

1. In a large saucepan, heat the ghee over medium heat. Sauté the onion, garlic, and celery for 5 minutes, until they begin to soften. Add the carrots, red pepper, sweet potato, and corn, and sauté for 3 minutes more.

2. Stir in the curry powder, lemon juice, cumin, and tumeric. Add 8 cups of water, stir, and cover. Bring the soup to a boil, cover, and simmer on low for 20 minutes.

3. Combine 2 cups of the soup broth with the cashews in a blender and blend on medium-high for 3 minutes, until very smooth.

4. Add the lentils and cashew puree to the soup and bring the soup back to a boil. Add the coconut milk and salt, and taste. You may add more salt or lemon juice to taste.

5. Serve hot, with a dollop of yogurt, and a sprinkle of chopped apples, coconut, and currants.

The Kitchen Goddess

Lakshman's Butternut Squash and Coconut Kitchari

Serves 4-6

Kitchari is one of the staple foods in Ayurveda, the ancient healing medicine of India. Simple, nourishing, and complete, kitchari contains complete protein, vegetables, and aromatic spices. This is one of our favorites.

2 T. ghee or olive oil

1 medium onion, sliced thinly

1 T. fennel seeds

1 t. ground cumin

1/2 t. tumeric

2 c. butternut squash, peeled and cubed into 1/2-inch pieces

1 c. golden mung dal, rinsed

1/2 c. basmati rice, rinsed

9 c. water

1 c. coconut milk

2 t. ground coriander

2 T. lemon juice

2 t. salt

1/4 c. fresh cilantro, chopped

1. In a large saucepan, heat the ghee over medium heat. Add the onions and sauté for 10 minutes, until very soft and golden brown. Add the fennel seeds, cumin, and tumeric and sauté for 2 minutes more.

2. Add the butternut squash, mung dal, rice, and water, and cover. Bring to a boil, lower the heat, and simmer over low heat for 45-60 minutes, until the dal and rice are very soft and dissolving. Stir occasionally.

3. Stir in the coconut milk, coriander, lemon juice, and salt. Heat through and serve hot with a sprinkle of fresh cilantro on top.

Ethiopian Lentil Stew Yemesir Wat

Serves 4

This spiced lentil stew is warming and grounding. Try it with Pita bread p. 118, or serve over rice or millet, an African grain.

1 c. green lentils

1 medium onion, minced

2 cloves garlic, minced

2 T. ghee

1/2 t. tumeric

1 t. minced fresh ginger

pinch cayenne pepper

2 t. cumin, ground

2 T. paprika

2 c. diced tomatoes

1/4 c. tomato paste

3 c. vegetable stock or water

1 c. green peas

2 t. salt

1 t. black pepper

1/4 c. fresh cilantro, chopped

1. Rinse the dry lentils in a colander and set aside.

2. In a stock pot, heat the ghee over medium heat. Sauté the onions and garlic in the ghee for 3-5 minutes, until translucent. Add the tumeric, ginger, cayenne, cumin, paprika, tomatoes, and tomato paste, and sauté, stirring often, for 2 minutes. Add the rinsed lentils and stir.

3. Pour in the stock or water and whisk to blend the soup. Bring the soup to a boil. Reduce the heat to low, cover, and simmer for 40-50 minutes, until the lentils are tender. Add the green peas, salt and pepper and cook for 5 more minutes. Garnish with chopped cilantro and serve with yogurt on the side.

The Kitchen Goddess

Thai Coconut-Ginger Soup

Serves 4-6

This soup is a favorite in the fall and winter, as the weather turns colder. It has the nourishing, homey quality of Mom's chicken soup, with an Asian kick of ginger!

1 t. light sesame oil

1 medium onion, diced

2 T. fresh ginger, minced

2 cloves garlic, minced

1/2 t. red chili flakes

1/2 c. red bell peppers, sliced

1/2 c. carrots, peeled and sliced long and thin

1/2 c. baby corn

7 c. water or vegetable stock

2 T. soy sauce

1/2 c. firm silken tofu, cut into 1/2 inch cubes

2 c. coconut milk

1 T. lemon juice

1 t. salt

1/4 c. fresh cilantro, chopped

1. In a large saucepan, heat the sesame oil over medium heat. Sauté the onion for 5 minutes, until translucent. Add the ginger, garlic, and red chili flakes, and sauté for two more minutes.

2. Stir in the bell peppers, carrots, and baby corn. Add the water and soy sauce, and gently stir in the silken tofu cubes. Cover and bring the soup to a boil. Lower the heat and simmer for 20 minutes.

3. Stir in the coconut milk, lemon juice, and salt. Heat through and serve hot, with a sprinkle of fresh cilantro.

"Embrace" by Faith Stone

"I met my Guru when I was very young. I was almost sixteen and still in school. I was rather bored with my studies, but I was very active in play. I was very good at playing. Gurudev [Nityananda] loved children, so whenever he came to our school all of us would leave our classes and follow him.

Whenever he came to my school, the teachers would be very upset, but the children would follow him anyway. He would go into a candy store, reach into the containers, throw candy to the children, and then take off again. Still, shopkeepers never complained, because whenever he gave away their candy, their sales went up."

– Swami Muktananda

Salads and Vegetable Side Dishes

Tomato, Cucumber, and Feta Salad   47

Panzanetta   48

Sesame Asparagus Salad   49

Marinated Broccoli and Summer Squash Salad   50

Almond Green Beans   51

Southern Style Smothered Collards   52

Fattouch Salad   53

Spinach Salad with Warm Miso Dressing   54

Black Sesame Yams   55

Calabacitas   56

Potato Pancakes with Homemade Applesauce   57

Indian-Style Mashed Potatoes   58

Shredded Citrus-Vegetable Salad   59

Tomato, Cucumber, and Feta Salad

Serves 4

This salad makes a delightful alternative to a green salad for Mediterranean meals. You can also serve it over a grain pilaf to make a simple meal in itself.

4 c. diced Roma tomatoes

2 c. cucumbers, peeled, seeded, and sliced in half-circles

2 c. feta cheese, cut into 1/2 inch cubes

1/4 c. extra-virgin olive oil

2 T. fresh lemon juice

1 t. fresh thyme or 1/2 t. dried thyme

1 t. fresh dill, chopped

1. Combine all ingredients in a medium mixing bowl and stir to combine. Allow the salad to marinate in the refrigerator for at least 30 minutes before eating.

2. Serve cold or at room temperature.

Panzanetta

This salad relies firmly on a good, crusty Italian bread. If you have leftover Italian bread, you can always cube and freeze it to save for this salad. It is worth the effort.

3 c. crusty Italian bread, white or wheat, cut into 1-inch cubes

3 c. diced Roma tomatoes

1/2 c. red onion, sliced very thin

1/2 c. extra-virgin olive oil

1/4 c. cider vinegar

1/2 c. fresh basil, sliced thinly

1 t. salt

1/2 t. black pepper

1. Preheat the oven to 450. In a mixing bowl, combine the bread cubes and 1/4 c. of the olive oil. Place the bread cubes on a baking sheet and toast them in the oven for 5-7 minutes, until crunchy on the outside, but still slightly soft on the inside. Remove from the oven and let the bread cubes cool completely.

2. In a medium mixing bowl, combine the tomatoes, red onion, 1/4 cup of olive oil, cider vinegar, basil, salt, and pepper. Stir to combine. Let the tomato mixture marinate in the refrigerator for at least 30 minutes.

3. Immediately before serving, stir the bread cubes into the tomato mixture. Taste the salad and add more salt and pepper, if desired.

The Kitchen Goddess

Sesame Asparagus Salad

Serves 4

This elegant salad has only one vegetable: asparagus. Beautifully presented, with a tangy sesame dressing, it is always a hit. In the springtime, when asparagus is perfect, serve this salad instead of a green salad.

20 medium stalks of asparagus

1/4 c. toasted sesame oil

2 T. tahini

1 T. soy sauce

1 T. red miso

1/4 c. warm water

1 T. lemon juice

1/2 t. fresh ginger, minced

1/4 c. toasted sesame seeds

1. Wash the asparagus and snap each stalk near the base; throw away the tough base of the stalk. Slice the asparagus in half lengthwise.

2. Heat one inch of water to boiling in a large saucepan. Steam the asparagus in the water for 3-4 minutes, until bright green and still crunchy. Remove the asparagus from the pan. Rinse the asparagus with cold water, and keep chilled while you assemble the dressing.

3. In a blender, combine the sesame oil, tahini, soy sauce, miso, warm water, lemon juice, and ginger. Blend on high until smooth and creamy.

4. Arrange the asparagus on four individual salad plates in a spiral. Using a ladle, drizzle the dressing over the top. Sprinkle with the toasted sesame seeds. Serve chilled.

Marinated Broccoli and Summer Squash Salad

Serves 4-6

In the summertime, cool marinated vegetables taste so good! This recipe is a no-fail crowd-pleaser during Shoshoni's busy summer season.

1 t. olive oil

1 medium onion, sliced into rings

1 red bell pepper, sliced thinly

1 c. yellow summer squash, sliced into rounds

3 c. broccoli florets

1/2 c. olive oil

2 T. cider vinegar

2 T. honey

1 T. fresh rosemary or 1 t. dried rosemary

1 T. fresh basil, thinly sliced

1 t. salt

1/4 t. black pepper

1. In a large skillet, heat 1 teaspoon of olive oil over medium heat. Sauté the onion in the olive oil for about 5 minutes, until it begins to brown. Stir in the red bell pepper and summer squash and sauté for 2-3 minutes more, until the vegetables begin to soften, but are still crunchy. Remove the skillet from the heat and transfer the vegetables to a plate. Let the vegetables cool.

2. Steam the broccoli for 3 minutes in a steamer or by placing it in a saucepan with one inch of boiling water. Remove the broccoli from the water and rinse it with cold water.

3. In a medium mixing bowl, whisk the olive oil, vinegar, honey, rosemary, basil, salt, and pepper. Stir in the cooled vegetables. Marinate the salad in the refrigerator for at least 30 minutes before serving. Serve cold or at room temperature.

The Kitchen Goddess

Almond Green Beans

This recipe is a favorite in the summer, when green beans grow in abundance. It is also a holiday favorite, a perfect complement to any special feast!

1 lb. green beans, washed and with the ends removed

1 medium onion, sliced in rounds

5 cloves garlic, sliced in halves

2 T. olive oil

1 T. fresh rosemary or 1 t. dried rosemary

1/2 t. dried sage

1/4 t. black pepper

1 1/2 t. salt

1/2 c. almonds, coarsely chopped

1. Preheat the oven to 400 degrees. Combine the green beans, onion, garlic, olive oil, rosemary, sage, pepper, and salt in a 9 x 13 inch baking dish. Stir to combine. Cover the dish with foil and bake for 30 minutes covered, then uncover and bake for 10 minutes more, until the green beans are tender but not soft, and lightly browned.

2. Place the almonds on a cookie sheet. Toast them in the oven for 10-15 minutes, until golden brown.

3. Stir the almonds into the green beans. Serve hot.

Southern Style Smothered Collards

Serves 4

This is our healthy take on a traditional Southern dish. The caramelized onion and slow-cooked tomatoes give the greens a delicious, rich flavor.

4 c. water

1 T. salt

1 bunch collard greens (about 10 large leaves), washed

2 T. olive oil

1 medium onion, cut in half and sliced into semi-circles

3 medium tomatoes, diced

1 t. dark molasses

1/2 t. dried sage

1/4 c. raw sunflower seeds

1 T. soy sauce

1 t. salt

1/4 t. black pepper

1. In a large saucepan, boil the water and salt. Remove the stems from the greens, and slice them into one-inch slices. Cook the greens in the boiling water for 5-10 minutes, until they are tender, not chewy. Drain the water, and rinse the greens with cool water.

2. In a large skillet, heat the olive oil over medium heat. Sauté the onions for 10 minutes, until very soft and golden brown. Add the tomatoes, molasses, and sage. Turn the heat to low, cover, and simmer for 10-15 minutes, until the tomatoes are soft and almost dissolving.

3. In a small skillet, toast the sunflower seeds over medium heat until golden brown. At the end, stir in the soy sauce to coat the seeds and remove from the heat.

4. Add the collards and sunflower seeds to the skillet with the tomato mixture. Add the salt and pepper and heat through. Serve hot.

The Kitchen Goddess

Fattouch Salad

This Lebanese salad, pronounced "fah-toosh," was a favorite at the Lebanese delis where I grew up. The large quantity of mint gives the salad a wonderful, refreshing taste!

Salad:

2 pita breads, white or whole wheat, sliced into 1-inch triangles

1 T. olive oil

2 hearts of Romaine lettuce, sliced 1 inch thick and washed

1/2 red onion, sliced thinly in half circles

1/2 c. kalamata or other black olives

Dressing:

1/2 c. olive oil

1/3 c. fresh lemon juice

2 T. honey

1/4 c. fresh mint, finely chopped, or 2 T. dried mint

2 t. oregano

1 t. salt

1/2 t. black pepper

1. Preheat the oven to 400 degrees. In a bowl, stir the olive oil and pita triangles together. Place them on a baking sheet, and toast them in the oven for 10 minutes, until crisp and golden brown. Remove from the oven and let the pita chips cool.

2. In a salad bowl, combine the lettuce, onion, and olives.

3. In a small bowl, combine the dressing ingredients and whisk to combine.

4. Toss the salad, dressing, and pita chips together immediately before serving. Serve cold.

Spinach Salad with Warm Miso Dressing

Serves 3-4

For this salad, the dressing is heated and tossed over the greens to wilt them, creating a salad that is both beautiful and easy to digest!

Salad:

2 bunches spinach, washed, stemmed, and dried

2 c. cherry tomatoes, sliced in half

1/2 yellow bell pepper, sliced thinly

1/2 c. sliced almonds

1/2 c. green apples, cut into 1 inch cubes

Dressing:

1/2 c. warm water

1/4 c. red miso

1/2 c. light sesame oil

1/4 c. rice vinegar

1/4 c. honey

2 T. tahini

1 T. light soy sauce

2 scallions, washed and diced

1 small clove garlic

1. In a salad bowl, combine the salad ingredients.

2. In a blender, combine the dressing ingredients and blend for 1-2 minutes, until very smooth.

3. Pour the dressing into a small saucepan and heat over medium heat, until just barely boiling. Remove from the heat and pour the dressing over the salad slowly, tossing the greens with tongs as you pour the dressing. Serve immediately.

The Kitchen Goddess

Black Sesame Yams

Serves 3-4

Black sesame seeds are available in most Asian grocery stores. They give this dish a distinctive appearance. The flavors go well with both Indian and Japanese meals.

4 large yams, peeled and sliced into half circles

2 T. dark sesame oil

1/4 c. black sesame seeds

1 1/2 t. salt

1. Preheat the oven to 400 degrees. In a 9 x 13 inch baking dish, combine the yams and the sesame oil. Stir to coat the yams with the oil. Cover the dish with foil, and bake for 25-30 minutes, until the yams are soft. Then uncover and bake for 5-10 more minutes, until the yams are golden brown.

2. Stir in the black sesame seeds and salt immediately before serving. Serve hot.

Calabacitas

This Mexican summer squash dish has a unique blend of ingredients. The feta cheese adds a pungent flavor that complements the mild squash.

1 T. cumin seeds

1 T. corn oil or canola oil

1 medium onion, sliced thin in

rounds

4 medium summer squash (zucchini or yellow squash) sliced into 1/4-inch thick rounds

1/2 c. crumbled feta cheese

1. Heat a large skillet over medium-high heat. Toast the cumin seeds for 3-5 minutes, until they turn golden brown and smell toasted.

2. Add the corn oil and onion slices, and sauté for 3 minutes, until the onions begin to soften. Add the summer squash, placing the slices flat in the pan. Sauté the squash slices for 2-3 minutes on each side, until both sides are golden brown.

3. Sprinkle the feta cheese over the top of the squash slices, cover the skillet, and turn the heat to low. Allow the squash to cook 2-3 minutes longer, until the cheese is just beginning to melt. Serve hot.

Potato Pancakes with Homemade Applesauce

Serves 4-6

This dish contrasts crispy, satisfying potatoes with cool, sweet applesauce. It is perfect for breakfast, as a side dish for a holiday meal, or for a simple dinner.

Pancakes:

2 large Russet potatoes, scrubbed

1 small onion

1 egg, beaten

1/4 c. whole wheat pastry flour

1/2 t. baking powder

1 t. salt

1/4 t. black pepper

1/2 c. olive oil

Applesauce:

4 large Granny Smith apples, cut into 1 inch cubes

1 cinnamon stick

3 whole cloves

1 c. water

1/4 c. maple syrup

pinch salt

1. In a medium saucepan, combine the applesauce ingredients. Heat over medium heat until the mixture boils. Lower the heat to low, cover, and simmer for 20 minutes, until the apples are soft. Remove the cinnamon stick and cloves and place the cooked apples and their juice in a food processor mixing bowl. Pulse 3-4 times, leaving the applesauce chunky. Refrigerate the applesauce while you make the pancakes.

2. Using a hand grater or the grating attachment of a food processor, grate the potatoes and onion. Place the shredded vegetables in a bowl, and stir in the egg, flour, baking powder, salt, and pepper.

3. Heat the olive oil in a medium cast-iron skillet over medium heat. Drop 2 tablespoons of the potato mixture into the oil and press to flatten with a spatula. Cook the pancakes for 5 minutes on each side, until golden brown. Place on a paper towel to cool. Serve warm with applesauce and a dollop of sour cream, if desired.

Indian-Style Mashed Potatoes

Serves 4-6

These curried sweet and white potatoes complement any Indian meal. Their spicy flavor and smooth texture make them an exciting change of pace.

2 medium Russet potatoes, peeled and cubed

2 medium yams, peeled and cubed

6 c. water

2 T. ghee or olive oil

2 cloves garlic, minced

1 T. fresh ginger, peeled and minced

1 T. curry powder

1 t. ground cumin

1 t. ground coriander

1 t. lemon juice

1/2 t. tumeric

1/2 t. cardamom

1/4 c. water

1/2 c. coconut milk

1 t. salt

1/4 c. fresh cilantro, chopped

1. In a large saucepan, boil the water. Add the potatoes and yams, cover, and boil for 20 minutes, until the potatoes are soft. Drain the water and place the potatoes in the bowl of a mixer or food processor.

2. In a medium skillet, heat the ghee over medium heat. Add the garlic and ginger and sauté for 2-3 minutes. Stir in the curry powder, cumin, coriander, lemon juice, tumeric, cardamom, and water. Sauté the spice mixture for 1-2 minutes longer.

3. Add the spice mixture, coconut milk, and salt to the potatoes. Using the beater attachment of the mixer, whip the potatoes for 2-3 minutes, until smooth.

4. Serve warm with a sprinkle of cilantro on top.

The Kitchen Goddess

Shredded Citrus-Vegetable Salad

This refreshing salad is perfect in the summertime. The crisp, cool texture of the vegetables and the sweet citrus enlivens Mexican and Jamaican meals. Jicama, a round root vegetable with a mild flavor and juicy texture, can be found in most grocery stores.

Salad:

1/2 medium jicama, peeled

1 medium carrot, peeled

1/2 green cabbage

1 c. sugar snap peas

2 medium tangerines or clementines, peeled and separated into sections

Dressing:

1/2 c. canola oil

2 T. lemon zest

1 clove garlic, minced

1/4 c. lime juice

2 T. honey

1 T. Dijon mustard

1 t. salt

1/4 t. white pepper

pinch clove powder

1. Using a grater or the grating attachment of a food processor, shred the jicama, carrot and cabbage into a medium salad bowl. Add the sugar snap peas and orange sections.

2. In a small skillet, heat the canola oil over medium heat. Add the lemon zest and garlic and heat for 1 minute more. Remove the oil from the heat and allow to cool completely.

3. In a small mixing bowl, whisk the oil, lemon zest, garlic, lime juice, honey, mustard, salt, pepper, and clove together. Pour the dressing over the salad and stir to combine. Refrigerate the salad for at least 20 minutes before serving. Serve cold.

"Lakshmi" by Faith Stone

"Once a poor man was sitting under a tree. For several days, he had had nothing to eat, and his stomach was beginning to give him trouble. In order to satisfy it, he began to cook in his imagination. First he cooked a rice dish, and then a vegetable, and then some soup. After he had finished cooking, he started to eat. He ate the soup and the rice, and then he ate the vegetable. But he had put too many chiles in the vegetable, and they burned his mouth. He began to fan his mouth, crying, 'Oooh, oooh!' Another man was sitting under a nearby tree, and when he saw this peculiar behavior he called out,

'Hey, brother, what's the matter with you?'

'I cooked some vegetables in my imagination, and I accidentally put in too many chiles!'

'You fool,' said the second man. 'Why did you put in so many chiles? Since you were only cooking in your imagination, couldn't you have made ice cream?'"

– Swami Muktananda

Grains, Beans, and Noodles

Wild Rice and Celery Root Casserole   63

Jasmine Fried Rice with Pineapple   64

Sesame Brown Rice   65

Kasha Varnishkes   66

Three-Bean Salad   67

Curry Kidney Beans with Homemade Cheese (*Panir*)   68

Chana Masala   70

Gingered Adzuki Beans   72

Sesame Soba Noodles   73

Cucumber-Rice Noodle Salad (*Sunomono*)   74

Polenta Squares with Eggplant Relish   75

French Lentil Salad   76

Tempeh Skillet   77

Tahini Barley Cereal   78

Coconut Cream of Wheat   79

Summer Fruit Muesli   80

Wild Rice and Celery Root Casserole

Serves 3-4

My mom often made a version of this casserole in the fall. The rich, nutty flavor of the wild rice is perfectly complemented by the creamy sauce.

Rice:

2 T. ghee or olive oil

1/2 medium onion, diced

1/2 medium celery root, peeled and minced

2 c. wild rice

4 c. water

1 t. salt

Sauce:

2 T. olive oil

2 T. unbleached flour

1/2 medium onion, diced

1 clove garlic, minced

1 stalk celery, minced

1/2 t. salt

1/2 t. black pepper

2 c. milk or plain soymilk

2 c. sharp cheddar cheese, grated

1. In a medium saucepan, heat the ghee over medium heat. Sauté the onion and celery root for 5-7 minutes, until very soft. Stir in the wild rice, water, and salt, and heat until boiling. Cover, reduce the heat to low, and simmer on low for 45-50 minutes, until the rice is tender. Remove from the heat and uncover.

2. Preheat the oven to 400 degrees. Oil a 9 x 13 inch baking pan.

3. In another medium saucepan, whisk the olive oil and flour together. Heat over medium heat until the mixture boils. Stir in the onion, garlic, and celery, and simmer the mixture for 3-5 minutes. Add the salt and pepper. Whisking constantly, add the milk a little at a time until it is all incorporated. Lower the heat to low, and bring the sauce to a boil, whisking occasionally. Stir in 1 cup of the cheese. Remove the sauce from the heat.

4. In a mixing bowl, combine the cooked rice and the sauce. Pour the mixture into the baking pan and sprinkle the remaining cheese on top. Cover with foil, and bake for 20 minutes covered. Uncover and bake for 15 minutes more. Serve hot.

Jasmine Fried Rice with Pineapple

Serves 4-6

Fragrant jasmine rice is full of flavor. You can find jasmine white rice and jasmine brown rice in many grocery stores and specialty food stores.

2 c. jasmine white or brown rice

3 1/2 c. water

2 T. sesame oil

1 T. fresh ginger, minced

2 cloves garlic, minced

1 c. sugar snap peas

1 c. fresh pineapple, cut into 1-inch cubes

2 T. red pepper, diced

2 T. light soy sauce

1/2 t. white pepper

1. Combine the rice and water in a medium pot and cover. Bring to a boil over medium high heat, then reduce the heat to low and simmer for 25 minutes (40 minutes for brown rice), until the rice is tender and the water is absorbed.

2. Spread the rice on a baking sheet to cool for 15-20 minutes.

3. In a large cast-iron skillet, heat the sesame oil over medium high heat. Add the ginger and garlic, and sauté for 2-3 minutes. Stir in the sugar snap peas, pineapple, and red pepper, and sauté for another 2-3 minutes. Add the cooled rice, soy sauce, and white pepper. Fry the rice for 5 minutes, turning carefully with a spatula.

4. Remove the rice from the skillet and serve hot.

The Kitchen Goddess

Sesame Brown Rice

Serves 4-6

This simple brown rice recipe is always a favorite. It complements any Asian meal.

1 T. dark sesame oil

2 c. short grain brown rice

4 c. water

1 t. salt

2 T. toasted sesame seeds

1. In a medium pot, heat the sesame oil over medium heat. Stir in the brown rice, coating it with the oil. Add the water, salt, and sesame seeds, and cover.

2. Bring to a boil over medium heat. Lower the heat and simmer for 35-40 minutes, until the rice is tender and the liquid is absorbed. Serve hot or room temperature.

Kasha Varnishkes

*This traditional Jewish dish, pronounced "**kah**-shah **var**-nish-kahs," is high in protein. Kasha is toasted buckwheat groats, available in most grocery and specialty food stores. The nutty flavor of the buckwheat perfectly complements the smooth pasta.*

2 T. ghee or olive oil

1 medium onion, minced

2 c. water or vegetable broth

1 c. kasha

2 t. salt

2 c. small bowtie pasta, cooked, drained, and rinsed with cool water

1. In a medium pan, heat the ghee over medium heat. Sauté the onion for 5-7 minutes, until it begins to caramelize. Cover, reduce the heat to low, and let the onions cook for 5 more minutes, until they are very soft and golden brown. Add the water and bring to a boil.

2. Stir in the kasha and salt, and cover. Bring to a boil, reduce the heat to low, cover, and simmer for 25 minutes, until the kasha is soft and fluffy.

3. Fluff the kasha with a fork, and stir in the pasta. Serve hot or room temperature.

Three-Bean Salad

Serves 4-6

A summer favorite, this bean salad combines the best of the garden's vegetables with cool, smooth beans. High in fiber and protein, it makes a nice accompaniment to picnic meals and sandwiches.

Salad:

2 c. water

2 c. green beans, ends trimmed

2 c. garbanzo beans, cooked and drained

2 c. adzuki beans, cooked and drained

1/2 red onion, sliced thinly in half circles

1 medium tomato, diced

1 yellow bell pepper, diced

Dressing:

1/2 c. olive oil

1/2 c. cider vinegar

4 T. maple syrup

2 T. red miso

2 T. light soy sauce

1 clove garlic, crushed

1/2 t. black pepper

1. In a medium pot, bring 2 cups of water to a boil. Add the green beans and steam them, covered, for 7-8 minutes, until tender, but still bright green. Drain, and rinse the green beans with cold water.

2. In a medium mixing bowl, stir the green beans together with the other salad ingredients.

3. In a small mixing bowl, whisk the dressing ingredients together. Pour the dressing over the salad and stir to mix. Refrigerate the salad for at least 30 minutes before serving. Serve cold.

Curry Kidney Beans with

Serves 4-6

Homemade cheese is such a treat, and it is very easy to make! All you need is organic whole milk and a little bit of courage. The results are amazing.

2 T. ghee or olive oil

1/2 medium onion, diced

1 clove garlic, minced

2 t. curry powder

1/2 t. tumeric

1 t. ground cumin

1 t. ground coriander

1/4 c. raw cashews

1 1/2 c. water

1 T. lemon juice

2 t. salt

4 c. kidney beans, cooked and drained

1 recipe Homemade Cheese, opposite page

1. In a large skillet, heat the ghee over medium heat. Sauté the onion and garlic for 2-3 minutes. Add the curry, tumeric, cumin, and coriander, and sauté for 2-3 minutes more.

2. Transfer the mixture to a blender and blend the spices together with the cashews, water, lemon juice, and salt. Blend for 3-4 minutes, until completely smooth.

3. Return the sauce to the pan. Stir in the kidney beans, and heat on medium heat until the mixture boils. Cover and simmer on low for 15 minutes.

4. Uncover the curry and stir in the Homemade Cheese. Serve immediately.

The Kitchen Goddess

Homemade Cheese
Panir

8 c. organic whole milk

2 T. white vinegar

cheesecloth

1 T. ghee

1. In a large pot, heat the milk over medium heat until it is just boiling. Turn the heat off, add the vinegar, and stir gently, once. Cover and let sit for 5 minutes. Place a piece of cheesecloth over a mesh strainer, on top of an empty pot. Pour the curds and whey through the cheesecloth.

2. Twist the top of the cheesecloth closed, creating a ball shape. Place the cheese onto a baking sheet. Place a heavy pot or pan on top of the cheese, and press down to squeeze out the water. Place the cheese in the refrigerator for 45 minutes to 1 hour, with the heavy pot on top.

3. Remove the cheese from the refrigerator and unwrap. It should be cold, and solidified to the texture of feta cheese or tofu.

4. Cut the panir into 1-inch cubes. Heat the ghee in a small skillet over medium heat. Place the panir cubes into the skillet, and fry, gently turning until all sides are golden brown. Remove from the heat.

Chana Masala

Serves 4

Making this recipe always reminds me of my sister, who loves Chana Masala! Spicy tomato masala (spice mixture) combines with nutty chickpeas for a perfect simple meal. Serve it with basmati rice.

1 T. ghee or olive oil

1 medium onion, diced

1 clove garlic, minced

1 t. tumeric

1 t. curry powder

1 t. ground cumin

1 t. ground coriander

1/2 t. paprika

1/4 t. cardamom, ground

4 medium tomatoes, diced

4 c. cooked chickpeas

1 T. lemon juice

2 t. salt

1 c. plain yogurt

1. In a large cast-iron pan, heat the ghee over medium heat. Sauté the onion and garlic for 2-3 minutes, until they begin to soften. Add the tumeric, curry, cumin, coriander, paprika, and cardamom, and sauté for 1-2 minutes more, stirring frequently.

2. Stir the tomatoes into the spice mixture, cover the pan, and reduce the heat to low. Simmer for 5-7 minutes, until the tomatoes are soft. Transfer the mixture to a blender and blend for 1-2 minutes, until the mixture is smooth. Return the spice mixture back to the pan.

3. Stir in the chickpeas, lemon juice, and salt. Bring the dish to a boil over low heat. Cover and simmer for 15 minutes. Serve hot, with a dollop of yogurt on top.

The Kitchen Goddess

Gingered Adzuki Beans

Serves 4-6

This comforting fall and winter stew is a simple Ayurvedic recipe. Serve it with chapatis, Pita bread, p. 118, or brown rice for a simple, grounding meal.

1 T. ghee or olive oil

3 T. fresh ginger, peeled and minced

2 t. cumin

2 t. coriander

2 c. adzuki beans, dry

8 c. water or vegetable broth

2 T. lemon juice

2 t. salt

2 T. cilantro, chopped

1. In a large pot, heat the ghee over medium heat. Sauté the ginger for 2-3 minutes, until it begins to soften. Add the cumin and coriander and sauté for 1-2 minutes more. Stir in the adzuki beans and water, and bring to a boil. Cover, lower the heat to low, and simmer for 75-85 minutes, until the beans are very soft.

2. Stir in the lemon juice and salt. Serve hot with a sprinkle of cilantro on top.

Saraswati, the Goddess of Speech, Education, and the Arts, in the Ma Shrine at Shoshoni Yoga Retreat.

Sesame Soba Noodles

Serves 4-6

Soba noodles are made from buckwheat, giving them a toasty flavor. They are widely available in grocery stores, and make a wonderful addition to Japanese meals. This versatile dish can be served cold, like a noodle salad, or hot, to accompany stir-fried vegetables. Try it with Spicy Asian Grilled Green Beans and Tofu, p. 95.

1/2 lb. soba noodles

16 c. water

1 t. salt

2 T. dark sesame oil

2 T. canola oil

1 T. fresh ginger, minced

1 clove garlic, crushed

1 T. rice vinegar

1/2 t. white pepper

2 T. hot water

1/2 c. dried shiitake mushrooms

1/4 c. toasted sesame seeds

1. In a large pot, bring the water and salt to a boil. Add the soba noodles and reduce the heat to medium. Boil for 5-7 minutes, until the noodles are tender but firm. Drain the noodles and rinse with cold water until cool.

2. In a medium bowl, whisk together the sesame oil, canola oil, ginger, garlic, rice vinegar, and white pepper. In another bowl, combine the dried shiitake mushrooms and hot water and let sit for 10 minutes. Drain the water from the mushrooms.

3. In a spice grinder, grind the sesame seeds to a fine powder. Stir the powder into the sesame oil mixture, and add the mushrooms. Toss the noodles together with the sauce. For cold noodles, refrigerate at least 30 minutes before serving. For hot noodles, heat a large skillet over medium heat. Sauté the noodle mixture for 5-7 minutes, tossing the noodles with tongs. Serve immediately.

Cucumber Rice Noodle Salad Sunomono

Serves 4-6

This crunchy, refreshing salad is perfect with any Japanese meal, or as a simple summer salad.

Salad:

1/2 lb. wide rice noodles

2 quarts boiling water

1 medium cucumber, peeled, seeded, and thinly sliced

1 red bell pepper, thinly sliced

1 medium carrot, thinly sliced

1 c. mung bean sprouts

1 T. black sesame seeds

Dressing:

2 T. light soy sauce

2 T. dark sesame oil

1 T. mirin rice wine

2 t. brown sugar or sucanat

1 clove garlic, crushed

1/2 t. white pepper

1. In a large pot, bring 2 quarts of water to a boil. Add the rice noodles, stir, and turn the heat off. Let the noodles sit in the water for 5-7 minutes, until tender but still firm.

2. Drain and rinse the noodles with cold water until very cold.

3. In a small bowl, whisk the dressing ingredients together.

4. In a large bowl, combine the noodles, cucumber, bell pepper, carrot, mung bean sprouts, black sesame seeds, and dressing. Toss with tongs to coat the noodles. Refrigerate at least 30 minutes before serving. Serve cold or room temperature.

Polenta Squares with Eggplant Relish

Serves 4

Polenta is simple, hearty Italian food that feels nourishing and homey when you eat it. Serve this dish with a loaf of Italian bread and a green salad, or serve as a side dish at your next Italian feast!

2 c. polenta

5 c. water

1T. salt

1/2 c. canola oil

<u>Relish:</u>

1 medium onion, diced

2 cloves garlic, mincedv

1/4 c. olive oil

1 t. oregano

1/2 t. red chili flakes

1 medium eggplant, peeled and cubed into 1/2-inch cubes

3 medium tomatoes, diced

3 T. fresh basil, sliced thinly

1 T. parsley, minced

1 1/2 t. salt

1/2 t. black pepper

1. Preheat the oven to 400 degrees. In a medium saucepan, bring the water to a boil. Stir in the polenta and salt. Turn the heat to low, and simmer over low heat, stirring frequently. Cook the polenta for 7-10 minutes, until the grains are soft and the mixture is very thick and hard to stir.

2. Remove from the heat and pour the polenta into an oiled 9x13-inch baking sheet. Smooth the top, and place the polenta in the refrigerator. Refrigerate for at least 45 minutes, until the polenta has completely cooled.

3. Meanwhile, in a 9x13 inch shallow baking dish, combine the onion, garlic, olive oil, oregano, chili flakes, and eggplant cubes. Toss to combine the ingredients. Cover with foil, and bake the eggplant for 25 minutes. Uncover, add the tomatoes, and bake for 15 minutes more. Remove from the oven and let cool for 15 minutes. Stir in the basil, parsley, salt, and pepper. Cover and keep at room temperature.

4. Take the polenta from the refrigerator and slice into 2 inch by 4 inch rectangles. In a medium cast iron skillet, heat the canola oil over medium heat. Fry the polenta squares for 5 minutes on each side, until golden brown. Remove with a slotted spoon and dry on paper towels.

5. Serve the polenta squares hot, with a scoop of eggplant relish on top. You can also top with parmesan cheese.

French Lentil Salad

Serves 4

Fresh herbs make this high-protein salad very special. If you have a garden, almost all the ingredients are in your backyard!

Salad:

4 c. cooked lentils

2 medium tomatoes, diced

1/2 red onion, finely diced

1/2 c. parsley, chopped

2 T. fresh basil, diced

1 T. fresh thyme leaves

1 t. rosemary leaves

Dressing:

1/4 c. olive oil

2 T. balsamic vinegar

1 T. honey

1 T. dijon mustard

1/2 t. black pepper

2 t. salt

1. In a medium bowl, combine the salad ingredients.

2. In a small bowl, whisk together the dressing ingredients.

3. Toss the dressing and the salad together, cover, and refrigerate for at least 30 minutes before serving. Serve cold or at room temperature.

The Kitchen Goddess

Tempeh Skillet

Serves 4

Excellent for breakfast or brunch, this easy meal-in-a-skillet is hearty and satisfying. You can find tempeh at most grocery stores and health food stores.

2 T. soy sauce

1 T. olive oil

1 T. honey

1 t. lemon juice

1 t. tomato paste

1 lb. plain tempeh

1 T. olive oil

1 medium onion, diced

1/2 green pepper, diced

1/2 red pepper, diced

1 medium potato, diced

1/2 t. thyme

1/2 t. basil

1/2 t. garlic powder

1/2 c. cheddar cheese, shredded

1. In a small bowl, whisk together the soy sauce, 1 T. of olive oil, honey, lemon juice, and tomato paste. Crumble the tempeh with your fingers and add to the bowl. Let sit for 15-20 minutes.

2. In a medium cast-iron skillet, heat 1 T. of olive oil over medium heat. Add the onion, green pepper, and red pepper, and sauté for 5-7 minutes until the vegetables are soft. Remove from the skillet and set aside in a bowl.

3. Add the potatoes, thyme, basil, and garlic powder to the skillet and sauté for 5-7 minutes, turning frequently to brown. Cover the skillet and cook for 10-12 minutes more.

4. Uncover the skillet and pour the tempeh and marinade in over the potatoes. Add the reserved onions and peppers. Cover the skillet, turn heat to low, and simmer for 10-12 minutes, until the tempeh has absorbed most of the liquid.

5. Uncover and sprinkle the cheese over the top of the mixture. Serve immediately.

Tahini Barley Cereal

Serves 6

This breakfast cereal has a nutty flavor. Warming for a winter day, it is also high in protein!

1/2 c. dry barley

8 c. water

1/2 c. tahini

1/2 c. maple syrup

1 t. vanilla

1 t. grated orange rind

1 t. salt

1. In a large saucepan, combine the barley and water. Bring to a boil over high heat, reduce the heat, cover, and simmer on low for 45 min-1 hour, until the barley is tender.

2. In a blender, combine half of the cooked barley, cooking water, tahini, maple syrup, vanilla, orange rind, and salt, and blend on medium until smooth, about 1-2 minutes.

3. Return the blended mixture to the pot and add the remaining cooked barley. Stir to combine. Heat over low heat until just boiling. Simmer for 5 minutes and serve hot.

The Kitchen Goddess

Coconut Cream of Wheat

This cereal is cooling and creamy. You can substitute cream of rice cereal if you have a sensitivity to wheat.

1/2 c. cream of wheat or cream of rice cereal

2 c. water

1/8 t. salt

3/4 c. coconut milk

3 T. sugar

1/2 t. vanilla

1. In a small cast-iron skillet, toast the cream of wheat dry over medium heat for 5-7 minutes, until golden brown. Remove from the heat.

2. In a small saucepan, combine the water and salt and bring to a boil over high heat. Turn the heat off and whisk in the cream of wheat. Continue whisking for 1 minute until the cereal thickens.

3. Stir in the coconut milk, sugar, and vanilla. Heat over low heat until the cereal just boils. Serve hot.

Summer Fruit Muesli

Always a favorite at summer breakfasts, muesli makes use of whatever fruits you have in season! You can make this recipe the night before for a very easy breakfast the next day!

2 c. rolled oats

1/2 c. rolled wheat or spelt flakes

1/2 c. almonds, ground

6 c. milk or plain soymilk

1 c. maple syrup

1 t. vanilla

pinch salt

3 c. fresh seasonal fruit, sliced: berries, peaches, bananas, apples (don't use citrus fruits)

1/2 c. sliced almonds

1. In a large mixing bowl, combine the oats, wheat flakes, and ground almonds. Stir to combine. You can add any other grain flakes that you like to this mix!

2. Add the milk, maple syrup, vanilla, and salt to the grains and stir to mix. Cover the bowl and place in the refrigerator for 2 hours or overnight.

3. In a small cast-iron skillet, toast the sliced almonds for 3-5 minutes, until golden brown. Remove from the heat and let cool.

4. Remove the muesli from the refrigerator. Stir in the fruit and nuts. Serve cold with extra milk, if desired.

"Vajra Sattva" by Faith Stone

"Vajra Yogini" by Faith Stone

"Chenrezig" by Faith Stone

"Green Tara" by Faith Stone

"Medicine Buddha" by Faith Stone

"Milarepa" by Faith Stone

"Ganesh with the Kids" by Faith Stone

"Visualize a ripe peach inside you, a ripe banana, a ripe papaya, and feel your heart open, feel the sweetness in yourself and allow that to flow."

– Swami Rudrananda

Entrees

Jamaican Jerk Tofu   89

Butternut Squash Lasagne   90

Angel Hair Pasta with Italian Salsa Fresca   91

Tofu Tikka Masala   92

Roasted Eggplant Curry   93

Tandoori Tempeh   94

Spicy Asian Grilled Green Beans & Tofu   95

Gorditas with Home Style Pinto Beans   96

Broccoli Strudel   98

Tostadas with Black Bean Refritos   99

Tofu Foo Yung with Mushroom Sauce   100

Whole Wheat Noodles with Asian Black Bean Sauce   102

Mushroom-Walnut Loaf   103

Summer Vegetable Pie   104

Pad Thai Style Vegetable Curry   105

Tofu Tacos with Tartar Sauce   106

Chili-Lime Baked Tofu   108

TVP Tacos   109

Tofu Parmesan with Carrot Marinara Sauce   110

Jamaican Jerk Tofu

This is one of the most popular tofu dishes we serve at Shoshoni. The citrus flavors combine with rich coconut milk for a wonderful Caribbean flavor. Serve with rice and peas, Coconut Bread, p. 116, and Avocado Slaw, p. 149.

2 lb. extra firm tofu

1 T. soy sauce

1 T. olive oil

Marinade:

1/2 c. lime juice

1/2 c. orange juice

1 green bell pepper, diced

3/4 c. water

1 t. basil

1/2 t. yellow mustard powder

1/2 t. thyme

1/8 t. allspice

1/8 t. ground cloves

1 1/2 c. coconut milk

1/4 c. cilantro, chopped

1 t. salt

1/2 t. red chili flakes

1/4 c. mango, cut into cubes

2 T. honey

1. Wrap the tofu blocks in a clean dish towel and place on a cutting board. Place a second cutting board on top of the tofu, and place a cast iron skillet or other heavy pot on top. Let the water press out of the tofu for 15-20 minutes.

2. Slice the tofu blocks crosswise into three squares. Then slice each square into two triangles. Sprinkle the soy sauce over the tofu.

3. Heat the olive oil in a large cast iron skillet over medium high heat. Fry the tofu for 3-5 minutes on each side, until golden and crunchy on the outside. Remove the tofu from the pan and place it in a shallow baking dish.

4. Preheat the oven to 375 degrees.

5. Combine the marinade ingredients in a blender and blend for 1-2 minutes, until smooth. Pour the marinade over the tofu in the baking dish. Bake for 30-40 minutes, until the sauce thickens and bubbles, and the tofu looks golden brown.

6. Serve hot, with Avocado Slaw on top.

Butternut Squash Lasagne

Serves 6

This lasagne is a perfect way to use fall squash, and is a wonderful alternative to traditional tomato-based Italian dishes. The flavors are savory and mild, making it a warming comfort dish.

Sauce:

2 medium butternut squashes, sliced in half lengthwise and seeded

1 head of garlic

2 T. olive oil

2 t. salt

6 c. water or vegetable stock

Filling:

1 T. olive oil

1 medium onion, diced

1 t. oregano

1 t. basil

1 t. rosemary

1/2 t. sage

1/4 t. black pepper

pinch nutmeg

4 c. ricotta or Tofu Feta, p. 145

1 1/2 c. mozzerella cheese, shredded

1/2 c. parmesan cheese

1/2 c. parsley, chopped

1 package lasagne noodles

1. Preheat the oven to 400 degrees. Oil a shallow baking dish. Place the squashes face down in the dish. Cut the top off the head of garlic, and place it face up in the pan by the squash. Drizzle the olive oil over the garlic head. Roast the squash and garlic for 35-45 minutes in the oven, until soft and golden brown. Remove from the oven and let cool.

2. In the meantime, heat the olive oil in a medium skillet over medium heat. Sauté the onion in the olive oil for 5 minutes, then add the oregano, basil, rosemary, sage, black pepper, and nutmeg. Remove the mixture from the heat and let cool.

3. In a mixing bowl, stir the onion mixture together with the ricotta cheese, 1 cup of the mozzerella, parmesean, and parsley.

4. When the squash has cooled, scoop the insides of the squash into a blender. Peel the roasted garlic cloves and add to the squash. Add the water and salt, and puree for 2-3 minutes until completely smooth.

5. Oil a deep 9 x 13 inch baking dish. Pour 1/2 c. of the sauce on the bottom of the pan. Layer uncooked lasagne noodles on top of the sauce. Then add 1/3 of the filling, followed by 1/4 of the remaining sauce. Repeat this process twice, until you have three layers of lasagne noodles. Pour the remaining 1/4 of the sauce on top. Cover with foil, and bake for 45 minutes. Uncover, sprinkle the top with the remaining 1/2 c. of mozzerella, and bake for 15 minutes more, until brown and bubbly. Serve hot.

The Kitchen Goddess

Angel Hair Pasta with Italian Salsa Fresca

This pasta dish is light and satisfying. For the olives, you can use canned black olives, or, for a special treat, use oil-cured black olives from the specialty foods store. For a traditional touch, serve with Italian bread and olive oil for dipping.

1 lb angel hair pasta or whole wheat angel hair pasta

2 quarts water

1 T. olive oil

<u>Salsa:</u>

6 medium Roma tomatoes, seeded and cut into 1/2 inch cubes

1 yellow tomato, seeded and cut into 1/2 inch cubes

1 c. black olives, sliced

1/2 red onion, minced

1 c. fresh basil, sliced

2 T. parsley, minced

3 T. olive oil

1 T. cider vinegar

1 t. salt

1/2 t. red chili flakes

1/2 t. oregano

1/2 t. black pepper

1. In a medium bowl, combine the salsa ingredients and stir to mix well. Cover and let sit at room temperature for at least 30 minutes.

2. In a medium pot, bring 2 quarts of water to a boil. Cook the pasta for 3-5 minutes, until tender but still firm. Drain, rinse with cool water, and toss with the olive oil.

3. Serve the pasta warm, with a scoop of the salsa on top. Grate some parmesan cheese on top for a special touch.

Tofu Tikka Masala

This mildly spiced Indian dish is a favorite at Shoshoni. The sauce is easily made ahead of time, and then you can assemble this dish in minutes. Serve with basmati rice and Naan bread, p. 120.

1 lb. extra firm tofu, cut into 1-inch cubes

2 T. olive oil

Sauce:

1 T. ghee

1 medium onion, diced

4 medium tomatoes, diced

2 T. tomato paste

1 T. fresh ginger, minced

2 t. curry powder (mild or hot)

2 t. cumin

1 t. salt

1 t. lemon juice

1 t. coriander

1/4 t. cardamom

1/4 t. tumeric

1/4 t. paprika

3/4 c. water

1 c. milk or plain soymilk

1 c. green peas, fresh or frozen

1/2 c. cilantro, chopped

1. In a medium cast-iron skillet, heat the olive oil over medium high heat. Sauté the tofu cubes for 3-4 minutes on each side, turning until the cubes are light brown and crispy. Remove from the heat and set aside.

2. In a large skillet, heat the ghee over medium heat. Sauté the onion for 5 minutes, until translucent. Add the tomatoes, tomato paste, fresh ginger, curry powder, cumin, salt, lemon juice, coriander, cardamom, tumeric, paprika, and water. Sauté the mixture on low heat for 5 minutes more, until it thickens and bubbles.

3. Transfer the spice mixture to a blender and blend for 1-2 minutes, until smooth. Return the mixture to the large skillet. Stir in the milk, peas, and tofu cubes. Bring the mixture to a boil over low heat, and simmer for 10-15 minutes. Serve hot, with a sprinkle of cilantro on top.

Roasted Eggplant Curry

Serves 4

This curry is known as a "dry" curry; rather than having a thick sauce, the spices are roasted, and then combined with vegetables for a delicious toasty flavor.

Spice Masala:

2 T. coriander seeds

1 T. cumin seeds

1 T. sesame seeds

1 t. black mustard seeds

1/2 t. fenugreek seeds

1/2 t. curry powder

2 black peppercorns

1 whole clove

3 T. olive oil

1 medium eggplant, peeled and cut into 1 inch cubes

2 c. green beans, ends removed and cut in half

1 medium onion, thinly sliced

1 t. salt

1/4 c. cilantro, chopped

1/2 c. plain yogurt

1. Preheat the oven to 400 degrees. In a small bowl, mix the coriander, cumin, sesame seeds, black mustard seeds, fenugreek, curry, black peppercorns, and clove. Heat a small cast iron skillet over medium heat, and place the spices in the dry pan. Toast the spices, stirring frequently, for 2-3 minutes, until they are browned and fragrant. The black mustard seeds will turn gray and start to pop like popcorn. Remove the spices from the heat and let cool.

2. Using a spice grinder or blender, grind the spices to a fine powder.

3. In a mixing bowl, combine the olive oil, eggplant, green beans, onion, and the spice powder. Pour the mixture into a 9 x 13 inch baking dish. Cover with foil and bake for 25 minutes. Uncover and bake for 10 minutes more, until the eggplant and green beans are tender. Stir in the salt and cilantro.

4. Serve hot with a dollop of yogurt.

Tandoori Tempeh

Serves 4

Traditionally, tandoori dishes are cooked in a wood fire oven. Our tempeh version is made in a traditional oven; using the broiler gives the tempeh a smoky flavor. Serve this dish with Basmati rice, or with a simple green salad.

1 lb. plain tempeh, sliced in half crosswise

2 T. light soy sauce

1 t. canola oil

Marinade:

2 T. tomato paste

2 T. water

1 T. molasses

1 t. paprika

1 t. coriander

1 t. cumin

1 t. lemon juice

1 t. salt

1/2 t. curry powder

1/4 t. tumeric

1/4 t. cayenne pepper

1 c. plain yogurt or soy yogurt

1. In a shallow 9x13-inch baking dish, sprinkle the soy sauce over the tempeh and let sit for 15 minutes.

2. Heat the canola oil in a large cast iron skillet over high heat. Sear the tempeh for 1-2 minutes on each side, until it develops a golden brown crust. Remove from the heat and return to the baking dish.

3. Preheat the broiler to 500 degrees. In a small bowl, combine the marinade ingredients and whisk together until smooth. Pour the marinade over the tempeh squares.

4. Cook the tempeh under the broiler for 10-15 minutes, until the sauce is bubbly and thickened. Remove from the oven and let cool. Cut the tempeh into long, thin strips. Serve hot with a dollop of yogurt on top.

The Kitchen Goddess

Spicy Asian Grilled Green Beans and Tofu

These green beans have a spicy kick and a delicious, crunchy texture from being stir-fried. They are perfect served with Sesame Brown Rice, p. 65.

1 t. canola oil

1 lb extra firm tofu, sliced crosswise into four pieces

2 T. soy sauce

1 T. sesame oil

1 medium onion, thinly sliced

1 red bell pepper, thinly sliced

6 c. green beans, ends cut off

Sauce:

2 T. dark sesame oil

2 T. sesame seeds

1 T. soy sauce

1/2 c. water

1 t. honey

1 t. red chili flakes

1 clove garlic, crushed

2 t. cornstarch

1. In a large cast iron skillet, heat the canola oil over medium high heat. Pan-fry the tofu for 5 minutes on each side, until it begins to brown. Sprinkle the soy sauce on the tofu. Remove from the heat and slice into long, thin slices.

2. In a small bowl, whisk together the sauce ingredients and set aside.

3. In the same large skillet or in a wok, heat 1 T. of the sesame oil over medium high heat. Sauté the onion, pepper, and green beans for 5 minutes, stirring constantly. Turn the heat down to medium and sauté for 3-5 minutes more. Pour the sauce on top, and stir to coat. Allow the sauce to begin to boil, then remove the vegetables from the heat. Stir in the tofu strips.

4. Serve hot with rice.

Gorditas with

Serves 4-6

Mexican food has always been a favorite at Shoshoni. Gorditas are made with masa harina, the same corn flour used to make tamales. You can find it in the Mexican food section of most grocery stores.

2 c. masa harina

1/2 c. all-purpose flour

1 t. salt

2 t. baking powder

1/4 c. canola oil

1 1/2 c. boiling water

canola oil for frying

1 recipe Home Style Pinto Beans, opposite page

1. In a mixing bowl, whisk the masa harina, flour, salt, and baking powder together. Stir in the canola oil until it is evenly distributed. Stirring constantly, add the boiling water until the mixture forms a very soft dough. Let the dough sit for 10 minutes.

2. In a large skillet, pour 1/2 inch of oil for pan frying. Heat the oil over medium heat. Form the masa dough into 2-inch wide patties, about 1/2 inch thick. Fry the patties for 5 minutes on each side, until golden brown on the outside and fluffy on the inside. Place them on a paper towel to dry.

3. Serve one or two gorditas in a bowl. Top with a ladle of Home Syle Pinto Beans, and a dollop of sour cream or yogurt. Serve hot.

Home Style Pinto Beans

2 c. dry pinto beans

8 c. water

1 T. canola oil or corn oil

1 medium onion, diced

4 medium tomatoes, diced

1/2 c. mild green chiles, diced

2 cloves garlic, crushed

1/2 jalepeno pepper, seeded
and minced

1/2 c. cilantro, chopped

2 t. salt

2 t. lemon juice

1. The night before, soak the pinto beans in a large bowl of cold water. Allow the beans to soak for at least 6 hours. (*for a faster version, you can use 4 c. canned cooked pinto beans and skip this step) Bring 8 c. of water to a boil in a large pot and add the soaked beans. Lower the heat, cover, and simmer for 85-100 minutes, until the beans are very soft. Drain most of the cooking water away, leaving about 2 cups of cooking liquid in with the beans.

2. In a large skillet, heat the canola oil over medium heat. Add the onion and sauté for 5 minutes. Add the tomatoes, green chiles, garlic, and jalepeno, and sauté for 5 minutes more. Cover, lower the heat, and simmer for 10 minutes.

3. Add the tomato mixture to the cooked beans. Stir in the cilantro, salt, and lemon juice. Serve hot.

Broccoli Strudel

Serves 4-6

This recipe was inspired by all our guests who love our spanakopeta! These delicate filo pastries are filled with broccoli and cheddar. You may substitute soy cheeses if you are sensitive to dairy.

1 package filo dough, thawed at room temperature

3 T. olive oil

1 T. butter, melted

1 medium onion, diced

1 clove garlic, minced

1 t. lemon juice

1/2 t. thyme

1/2 t. oregano

5 c. broccoli florets

1 c. ricotta cheese

1 c. sharp cheddar cheese, grated

2 T. parmesean cheese

1 t. salt

1/2 t. black pepper

1/2 c. plain yogurt

1. In a medium saucepan, heat one tablespoon of the olive oil over medium heat. Sauté the onion and garlic for 5 minutes. Add the lemon juice, thyme, oregano, and broccoli. Cover the pan and let steam for 5-7 minutes, until the broccoli is bright green, but not soft.

2. Transfer the broccoli mixture to a food processor with a blade attachment. Pulse the vegetables until they are minced into small pieces.

3. In a medium bowl, combine the broccoli mixture with the ricotta, cheddar, parmesan, salt, and pepper.

4. Preheat the oven to 400 degrees. Combine the melted butter and 2 T. of olive oil in a small bowl and set aside.

5. Roll out one sheet of filo dough. Using a pastry brush, brush the filo lightly with the oil mixture, and then lay another sheet on top. Repeat this nine times, for a total of ten sheets of filo. Place half of the broccoli mixture on the filo, and spread it out over the sheet evenly, leaving one inch of space at the end of the filo sheet. Roll up the filo sheet the short way and place on a cookie sheet. Slice the filo roll into 1-inch thick slices using a serrated knife.

6. Repeat with the other half of the filo dough and filling.

7. Bake the strudel as a roll for 25-30 minutes, until golden brown and crunchy. Serve the slices hot, with a dollop of plain yogurt.

The Kitchen Goddess

Tostadas with Black Bean Refritos

Serves 4

Tostadas are the perfect food to share with friends and family. We serve tostadas with a variety of different toppings, so everyone is happy!

12 corn tortillas

1 c. canola oil for frying

1 t. salt

1 lime, sliced in half

Black Bean Refritos:

3 c. black beans

12 c. water

2 T. olive oil

1 medium onion, diced

2 t. lemon juice

1 t. cumin

2 t. salt

Toppings:

Shredded cheddar cheese

Mashed avocado

Yogurt or sour cream

Red or green salsa

Black olives

Scallions

Sweet corn

Shredded lettuce

Cilantro

1. The night before, soak the black beans in a large bowl of cold water. Soak the beans for at least 6 hours.

2. In a large pot, heat the water to boiling and add the black beans. Lower the heat, cover, and simmer for 90-100 minutes, until the beans are very soft. Drain the water from the beans.

3. In a small skillet, heat the olive oil over medium heat. Add the onion and sauté for 5 minutes, until translucent. Add the lemon juice, cumin, and salt.

4. In a food processor, combine the cooked beans with the onion mixture. Pulse several times to combine, leaving the mixture chunky. Cover and set aside.

5. In a medium cast-iron skillet, heat the oil over medium high heat. Fry each corn tortilla for about 5 minutes, until crunchy and light brown in color. Remove with tongs and dry on a paper towel. When cool, sprinkle the tostada shells with salt and lime juice.

6. Serve the tostadas like a salad bar, with all the toppings in little bowls for people to assemble their own. Place about 1/4 c. of the refried beans on each tostada shell. Arrange toppings on top however you like!

Tofu Foo Yung with

These little tofu patties go well with any Asian meal. They have a delicate, soft texture and sesame flavor. Kids love them, too! Try serving with Whole Wheat Noodles with Asian Black Bean Sauce, p. 102.

1 lb. firm tofu

2 T. soy sauce

2 T. whole wheat pastry flour

1 T. nutritional yeast

2 t. dark sesame oil

1 t. salt

1/2 t. garlic powder

2 stalks celery, finely chopped

1/2 medium onion, finely chopped

2 T. canola oil

1 recipe Mushroom Sauce, opposite page

1. Place the tofu in a food processor with bowl attachment. Process until the tofu forms a smooth paste. Add the soy sauce, pastry flour, nutritional yeast, sesame oil, salt, garlic powder, celery, and onion, and process for 1-2 minutes more. Transfer the mixture to a bowl.

2. In a medium skillet, heat the canola oil over medium heat. Drop the tofu mixture by spoonfuls into the skillet, and then flatten them into small patties, about 3 inches in diameter. Fry the patties for 3-5 minutes on each side, until golden brown and crisp. Remove from the heat.

3. Serve the foo yung patties with a ladle of Mushroom Sauce on top. Serve hot.

Mushroom Sauce

1/4 c. soy sauce

1 c. water

2 t. dark sesame oil

2 T. corn starch

1 t. rice vinegar

1 t. ginger, powdered

1 t. brown sugar or sucanat

1 clove garlic, crushed

1 c. mushrooms, button or
   shitake, sliced thinly

1. In a small saucepan, whisk together all of the sauce ingredients except the mushrooms. Place the saucepan over low heat, and heat to boiling, stirring constantly. Once the mixture boils, add the mushrooms, cover, and simmer for 5-7 minutes more, until the mushrooms are tender and the sauce is thickened.

2. Remove from the heat and serve immediately.

Whole Wheat Noodles with Asian Black Bean Sauce

Serves 4-6

Black bean sauce, a traditional Chinese and Korean menu item, is full of protein and flavor! This dish works well as a main dish or special side dish.

1 lb whole wheat spaghetti

2 quarts water

1 T. light sesame oil

1 clove garlic, crushed

1 T. fresh ginger, minced

3 T. soy sauce

1/2 t. red chili flakes

1 c. black beans, cooked

2 c. cold water or vegetable broth

2 T. canola oil

1 T. red miso

1 T. rice vinegar

1 T. corn starch

1. In a medium bowl, mash the black beans with a potato masher. Add the garlic, ginger, soy sauce, red chili flakes, water, canola oil, miso, vinegar, and corn starch. Whisk the sauce together until ingredients are blended.

2. Transfer the sauce to a medium saucepan. Heat the sauce over medium heat until it begins to boil, whisking occasionally. Lower the heat and simmer the sauce for 5-7 minutes. Remove from the heat.

3. In a large pot, boil 2 quarts of water. Cook the whole wheat spaghetti for 7-10 minutes, until tender but still firm. Remove from heat, drain, and rinse with cold water. Toss with sesame oil.

4. Pour the sauce over the noodles, toss to coat, and serve immediately.

The Kitchen Goddess

Mushroom-Walnut Loaf

This dish makes a wonderful warming winter meal. Served with mashed potatoes and our vegetarian Homestyle Gravy, p. 147 it is comforting, savory, and fulfilling.

1 T. olive oil

1 medium onion, diced

1 clove garlic, minced

1 c. mushrooms, sliced

1 t. thyme

1 t. rosemary

1/2 t. oregano

1/2 t. black pepper

1 t. salt

2 c. walnuts

2 c. brown rice, cooked

1 c. cottage cheese

1 c. grated cheddar cheese

1/2 c. parmesan cheese

3 eggs

1. Preheat the oven to 375 degrees. In a large skillet, heat the olive oil over medium heat. Sauté the onion and garlic for 5 minutes. Add the mushrooms, thyme, rosemary, oregano, black pepper, and salt, and sauté for 5 minutes more. Remove from the heat.

2. In a food processor with bowl attachment, process the walnuts until they resemble bread crumbs.

3. In a large mixing bowl, combine the brown rice, walnuts, and mushroom mixture. Stir in the cottage cheese, 3/4 cup of the cheddar cheese, and parmesan. In a small bowl, beat the eggs until smooth; add the eggs to the rice mixture and stir to combine.

4. Oil a large loaf pan. Pour the rice and mushroom mixture into the pan. Cover with foil and bake for 50 minutes covered. Uncover, sprinkle the top with the remaining cheddar cheese, and bake for 10 minutes more.

5. Remove from the oven and let cool for 15 minutes before slicing. Slice the loaf into 6 or 7 pieces. Serve hot, with gravy if desired.

Summer Vegetable Pie

Serves 4-6

This pie lends itself to many variations. In the summer, when the garden is in full bloom, use your favorite vegetables to create this light, flaky pie. Served with a green salad, it makes a satisfying dinner.

1 package filo dough, thawed

2 T. olive oil

1 medium onion, diced

1 zucchini, sliced thinly in rounds

1 yellow summer squash, sliced thinly in rounds

1 red pepper, sliced

1 medium tomato, sliced in rounds

1/2 c. mushrooms, sliced

2 T. olive oil

1 t. thyme

1 t. savory

1 t. marjoram

1 t. salt

1/2 t. black pepper

1. Preheat the oven to 400 degrees. Oil a deep dish pie pan. Pour the olive oil into a small bowl with a pastry brush for the filo dough. Unroll the filo dough, and trim the sheets across the short end, so that the sheets form an 8-inch by 8-inch square.

2. Place one sheet of filo in the pie pan, brush the top with olive oil, and lay another sheet of filo on top, turning the square 90 degrees so that the corners of the squares do not overlap. Repeat 14 times, until you have 15 sheets of filo on the bottom of the pan.

3. Bake the filo for 10-12 minutes, until light brown and crisp. Remove from the oven and let cool for 10 minutes.

4. In a small bowl, combine the thyme, savory, marjoram, salt and pepper.

5. Arrange the vegetables on the crust in 3 layers: onions and zucchini; summer squash and red peppers; tomatoes and mushrooms. On top of each layer, drizzle a little bit of the olive oil and sprinkle 1/3 of the herb mixture.

6. Bake the pie in the oven for 25 minutes, until the vegetables are tender, yet still crisp. Serve hot or room temperature.

The Kitchen Goddess

Pad Thai Style Vegetable Curry

Serves 3-4

Always a flavorful favorite, Pad Thai makes an appearance on our table sometimes as a delicious vegetable curry! You can increase the red chilis to make this as spicy as you like.

Sauce:

1 T. dark sesame oil

1 clove garlic, minced

1 t. ginger, minced

2 T. rice vinegar

3 T. brown sugar or sucanat

3 T. soy sauce

2 T. water

1 T. corn starch

1 t. salt

1/2 t. red chili flakes

1 T. toasted sesame oil

1 medium onion, sliced thinly

1 red pepper, sliced

1/2 green pepper, sliced

1/2 head of cauliflower, chopped into florets

1/4 green cabbage, sliced

1/2 lb. mung bean sprouts

3 T. peanuts, crushed

1/2 c. cilantro

1 lime, cut into wedges

1. In a medium saucepan, heat the sesame oil over medium heat. Add the garlic and ginger and sauté for 1-2 minutes.

2. In a separate bowl, combine the rice vinegar, brown sugar, soy sauce, water, corn starch, salt, and red chili flakes. Pour this mixture into the saucepan, and bring to a boil, whisking constantly. Remove from the heat.

3. In a large cast-iron skillet, heat 1 T. sesame oil over medium-high heat. Sauté onions for 1-2 minutes, until they begin to brown. Add red pepper, green pepper, and cauliflower, and sauté for 2-3 minutes more. Turn down the heat to low, add the cabbage, cover, and steam the vegetables for 5-7 minutes.

4. Uncover the pan, stir the vegetables, and add the bean sprouts. Pour the sauce over the vegetables and stir to combine.

5. Serve vegetables in individual bowls with a sprinkle of peanuts, cilantro, and a lime wedge. Serve with rice or noodles on the side, if desired. Serve immediately.

Tofu Tacos with

These tacos remind me of summers at the beach. They are as delicious as they are fun to eat! Try them with a marinated vegetable salad like Marinated Broccoli and Summer Squash Salad, p. 50.

1 lb. firm tofu, sliced into 10 rectangles

3 T. soy sauce

1/2 c. corn meal

1/2 c. whole wheat pastry or white flour

1/2 t. oregano

1/2 t. paprika

1/2 t. garlic powder

1 t. salt

1/2 t. black pepper

1/2 c. canola oil

10 corn tortillas

1/2 green cabbage, shredded

1 recipe Vegan Tartar Sauce, opposite page

1. Pour the soy sauce into a small mixing bowl. In a medium mixing bowl, combine the corn meal, flour, oregano, paprika, garlic powder, salt, and pepper.

2. In a large cast iron skillet, heat the canola oil over medium high heat. Dip the tofu pieces in the soy sauce first, then into the corn meal mixture, coating them completely. Fry them in the oil for 3 minutes on each side, until golden brown. Remove from the oil and place on a paper towel to cool.

3. Dip the tortillas one at a time into the hot oil for about 30 seconds each, until they bubble, but do not become crunchy. Remove the tortillas from the oil and drain on paper towels.

4. To assemble the tacos, place one piece of tofu inside each corn tortilla. Add a sprinkle of shredded cabbage and a dollop of Vegan Tartar Sauce on top. Serve immediately.

Vegan Tartar Sauce

1 lb. firm silken tofu

1 T. lemon juice

1 t. salt

1/2 t. garlic powder

1/2 t. honey

1/4 white onion, finely minced

1/4 c. pickle relish

1. In a food processor, blend the silken tofu until completely smooth. Add in the lemon juice, salt, garlic powder, honey, onion, and pickle relish. Pulse 2 to 3 times, until combined.

2. Cover and refrigerate in a small bowl.

Chili-Lime Baked Tofu

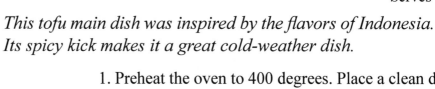

Serves 3-4

This tofu main dish was inspired by the flavors of Indonesia. Its spicy kick makes it a great cold-weather dish.

1 lb firm tofu

1/4 c. sesame oil

1 quart water

Sauce:

1 T. dark sesame oil

1 medium onion, chopped

2 medium tomatoes, chopped

1 clove garlic, minced

1 t. red chili paste

6 T. tomato paste

3 c. water or vegetable stock

1/4 c. lime juice

1/4 c. honey

1/4 c. soy sauce

1 t. lime zest

1 t. salt

1/2 t. garlic powder

1/4 t. white pepper

1. Preheat the oven to 400 degrees. Place a clean dish towel on a cutting board. Place the tofu on the dish towel, and layer another towel on top of the tofu. Put another cutting board on top, and then place something heavy, like a large pot, on the top cutting board. Press the tofu for 15 minutes.

2. Slice the tofu into 1-inch cubes. In a large cast iron skillet, heat the sesame oil on medium high heat. Fry the tofu for about 3 minutes on each side, until golden brown and crunchy on the outside.

3. In a medium saucepan, bring 1 quart of water to a boil. Add the fried tofu cubes, and boil them for 2-3 minutes. Drain the water from the tofu cubes.

4. To prepare the sauce, heat 1 T. sesame oil in a medium saucepan over medium heat. Add the onions, tomatoes, and garlic, and sauté for about 5 minutes, until the onions start to look translucent. Add the chili paste, tomato paste, water, lime juice, honey, soy sauce, lime zest, salt, and garlic powder, and whisk together to incorporate all ingredients. Bring to a boil over medium heat, reduce heat, cover, and simmer for 10 minutes. Transfer the sauce to a blender.

5. Blend the sauce in the blender until smooth. Add the white pepper.

6. Place the tofu cubes in a shallow baking dish. Pour the sauce on top and bake uncovered for 20-25 minutes, until the sauce is bubbling. Serve hot with steamed rice.

The Kitchen Goddess

TVP Tacos

Serves 4-6

These tacos are easy to make and always a crowd pleaser. TVP, available in most health food stores, has lots of protein and very little fat!

2 c. dry TVP

2 c. boiling water

1 T. olive oil

1 medium onion, diced

1 t. ground cumin

1 T. mild chili powder

1/2 t. oregano

2 T. tomato paste

1 T. soy sauce

2 t. lemon juice

2 t. salt

12 taco shells

<u>Toppings:</u>

Shredded lettuce

Shredded cheese

Diced tomatoes

Sliced scallions

1. In a small mixing bowl, combine the TVP and boiling water. Let stand for 15 minutes, until the water is all absorbed.

2. In a medium skillet, heat the olive oil over medium heat. Add the onion and sauté for 5 minutes, or until translucent. Add the cumin, chili powder, oregano, tomato paste, soy sauce, and lemon juice and stir to combine. Sauté for 1-2 minutes more.

3. Add the TVP to the skillet and stir to combine all ingredients. Cover and turn the heat to low. Simmer for 15 minutes. Uncover, add the salt, and remove from the heat.

4. Preheat the oven to 400. Toast the taco shells for 3-4 minutes. Remove from the oven and place 2-3 T. of TVP filling in each taco shell. Top with toppings and serve immediately.

Tofu Parmesan with

Serves 4

Tofu Parmesan is a delicious way to enjoy tofu Italian style! Making the marinara sauce with carrots reduces the acidity of the sauce. It is easier to digest, as well as full of vitamins!

1 lb firm tofu

3 T. soy sauce

1/4 c. corn meal

1/4 c. parmesan cheese

1/2 c. whole wheat pastry flour

1/2 t. oregano

1/2 t. basil

1/2 t. rosemary

1/2 t. garlic powder

1 t. salt

1/2 t. red chili flakes

1/2 c. canola oil

1 recipe Carrot Marinara Sauce, opposite page

1. Slice the tofu into about 9 rectangles. In a small bowl, have the soy sauce ready. In another small bowl, combine the corn meal, parmesan cheese, flour, oregano, basil, rosemary, garlic powder, salt, and chili flakes.

2. In a large cast iron skillet, heat the canola oil over medium high heat. Dip the pieces of tofu in the soy sauce, then in the flour mixture, coating both sides. Fry the coated tofu pieces in the oil for about 5 minutes on each side, until golden brown. Remove from the pan and dry on paper towels.

3. Serve the tofu pieces hot, with Carrot Marinara sauce, and pasta, if desired.

The Kitchen Goddess

Carrot Marinara Sauce

Serves 4-6

Carrot Marinara:

1 T. olive oil

1 medium onion, diced

2 cloves garlic, minced

1 t. basil

1 t. oregano

1/2 t. rosemary

1/2 t. red chili flakes

6 large carrots, peeled and chopped

4 Roma tomatoes, diced

1 T. tomato paste

4 c. water

2 t. salt

1. In a large saucepan, heat the olive oil over medium heat. Sauté the onion and garlic for about 5 minutes, until translucent. Add the basil, oregano, rosemary, and chili flakes, and sauté for 2-3 minutes longer.

2. Add the carrots, tomatoes, tomato paste, and water to the pot. Cover and bring to a boil. Reduce heat and simmer for about 45 minutes, until the carrots are very soft.

3. Blend the sauce in a blender until smooth. Return to the pot and add the salt. Cover and simmer the sauce on low heat for 30-40 minutes, stirring occasionally. Serve hot.

"Shiva and Parvati" by Faith Stone

"It really is like walking into a grocery store. In the produce section all the vegetables are laid out. You have all this material and you run to a rotten tomato, a rotten cabbage, and you say, 'Oh, this is what I am.' Yes, that's true. Part of that is you. But if you go to a fresh and beautiful tomato and beautiful cabbage and you put your love and attention there, that will be what you smell. "

– Swami Rudrananda

Bakery

Sweet Potato Spice Bread   115

Coconut Bread   116

Maple-Walnut Quick Bread   117

Pita Bread   118

Poori Bread   119

Naan Bread   120

Potato Knishes   121

Whole Grain Bagels   122

Chocolate-Cinnamon Babke   124

Triple Berry Muffins   126

Molasses Rye Bread   127

Banana Pancakes   128

English Muffins   129

Sweet Potato Spice Bread

Serves 6-8

This has become a favorite bread at Shoshoni over the years!
Every time we make it, people ask for the recipe.

3/4 c. unbleached flour

3/4 c. whole wheat pastry flour

1 t. baking soda

1/4 t. baking powder

1 t. salt

2 t. cinnamon

3/4 t. ground ginger

1/2 t. ground nutmeg

1/4 t. ground cloves

1/3 c. plain yogurt

1/2 t. vanilla

6 T. melted butter or canola oil

1 1/4 c. brown sugar or sucanat

2 eggs, beaten

1 c. cooked sweet potato, pureed

1. Preheat oven to 375 degrees. Oil and flour a 9x5 inch loaf pan.

2. In a medium bowl, combine the flour, baking soda, baking powder, salt, cinnamon, ginger, nutmeg, and cloves. Whisk the dry ingredients together.

3. In another medium mixing bowl, whisk together the yogurt, vanilla, melted butter, brown sugar, and eggs. Fold in the pureed sweet potato.

4. Stir the flour mixture into the wet ingredients, stirring until just combined. The mixture may have a few small lumps left.

5. Pour the batter into the loaf pan and bake for 50 min. - 1 hour, until a toothpick inserted in the center comes out clean.

6. Remove from the oven and let cool thoroughly before slicing.

Coconut Bread

Serves 6-8

For coconut lovers, there is no tastier treat than fresh Coconut Bread! This bread goes well with Jamaican Jerk Tofu, p. 89.

3 c. unbleached flour

1/2 c. sugar or sucanat

2 t. baking powder

1/4 t. salt

1 egg, beaten

1 1/2 c. canned coconut milk

3/4 c. milk or plain soymilk

1/2 c. canola oil

1 t. vanilla

2 c. grated unsweetened coconut

1. Preheat the oven to 375 degrees. Oil and flour a 9x5 inch loaf pan.

2. In a medium mixing bowl, combine the flour, sugar, baking powder, and salt.

3. In another medium mixing bowl, whisk together the egg, coconut milk, milk, canola oil, and vanilla. Stir in the coconut.

4. Stir the flour mixture into the wet ingredients, being careful not to over-mix. Stir until just combined.

5. Pour the batter into the loaf pan and bake for 50 min. - 1 hour, until a toothpick inserted in the center comes out clean.

6. Remove from the oven and let cool thoroughly before slicing.

The Kitchen Goddess

Maple-Walnut Quick Bread

Serves 6-8

A homey classic, this bread is sweetened only with maple syrup and applesauce.

1 1/2 c. unbleached flour

1 c. whole wheat pastry flour

1 T. baking powder

1/2 t. salt

1 c. milk or soymilk

3/4 c. maple syrup

1/4 c. applesauce

3 T. canola oil

1 t. vanilla

1 c. walnuts, chopped

1. Preheat the oven to 375 degrees. Oil and flour a 9x5 inch loaf pan.

2. In a medium mixing bowl, combine the flour, baking powder, and salt. Whisk together until combined.

3. In another mixing bowl, whisk together the milk, maple syrup, applesauce, canola oil, and vanilla.

4. Stir the flour mixture into the wet ingredients until just combined. Fold in the walnuts.

5. Pour the batter into the loaf pan and bake for 50 min. – 1 hour, until a toothpick inserted in the center comes out clean.

6. Remove from the oven and let cool thoroughly before slicing.

Pita Bread

Who makes their own pita bread, you wonder? You do! It's easier than it seems, and the results are well worth the small amount of extra time. If you have any left over, you can toast triangles in the oven to make pita chips.

1 T. dried yeast

2 c. warm water

2 t. honey

5 c. unbleached white flour

2 t. salt

extra flour for rolling out

1. In a small bowl, combine the yeast, warm water, and honey. Whisk thoroughly, and let stand for 10-15 minutes, until the yeast begins to bubble.

2. Stir the flour and salt into the yeast mixture until combined. Flour a countertop, turn the dough onto it, and knead the dough for 5-10 minutes, until it is smooth and elastic.

3. Place the dough in a clean bowl, cover with a dish towel, and place in a warm spot. Let rise for 30-40 minutes, until doubled in size.

4. Preheat the oven to 500 degrees. Place a large cookie sheet in the oven as it preheats.

5. On a floured countertop, divide the dough into 12-15 small balls. Flatten each ball into a disk. Using a rolling pin, roll each ball out to 1/4 inch thick.

6. Using a spatula, place the pita breads on the preheated cookie sheet in the oven. You may have to bake the breads in 2-3 batches.

7. Bake for 3-5 minutes, until the breads puff up, but do not get crunchy. Use a spatula to remove the breads from the oven to cool.

8. Slice breads in half and stuff with your favorite sandwich filling, or cut into triangles and serve with any dip!

The Kitchen Goddess

Poori Bread

Another long-standing favorite at Shoshoni, poori bread are a classic bread of Indian cuisine. The perfect poori puffs up into a little golden balloon when fried. Serve these breads as an accompaniment to any Indian or Thai dish.

1 c. whole wheat flour

1 c. unbleached white flour

1/2 t. salt

2 T. ghee or melted butter

1/2-3/4 c. warm water

2 c. canola oil for frying

1. In a small bowl, combine the whole wheat flour, unbleached white flour, and salt. Stir in the ghee or butter, mixing until the mixture resembles a coarse meal.

2. Slowly add the water to the flour mixture, stirring to combine. Add just enough water to form a soft dough.

3. Turn the dough out onto a floured countertop and knead for 5 minutes, until very smooth. Place the dough into a bowl, cover, and let rest for 15 minutes.

4. In a medium cast-iron skillet, heat the canola oil over medium heat. Divide the poori dough into 16 small balls.

5. Roll each poori out until it is about 4 inches in diameter and 1/8 inch thick.

6. Slide the pooris one at time into the hot oil. When the poori rises to the surface, use a spoon to hold it gently under the surface until it puffs up. Fry for about 1 minute on each side. Remove from the oil with a slotted spoon and drain on paper towels.

7. Serve immediately.

Naan Bread

We had to include this flat bread in our collection, because it is so delicious and easy to make. Though it is traditionally baked in a tandoori oven, we use a flat iron griddle and it comes out fabulous.

1 T. dried yeast

1 1/2 c. water

1/4 c. honey

1 c. plain yogurt

1/2 c. ghee or melted butter

5 c. unbleached flour

1 t. salt

extra ghee, melted

1. In a small bowl, combine the yeast, water, and honey. Whisk together until thoroughly combined, and then let sit for about 15 minutes, until the yeast begins to bubble.

2. Stir the yogurt and ghee into the yeast mixture. Add the flour and salt and stir to combine.

3. Turn the dough onto a floured board and knead for 7-10 minutes, until very smooth and elastic. Place the dough in a bowl, cover with a dish towel, and place in a warm location. Let rise for 45 minutes.

4. Heat a flat griddle to medium-high heat. On a floured cutting board, divide the dough in half. Roll out each half of the naan into a large circle or oval, about 10 inches in diameter and 1/4 inch thick. You can also roll out small, individual-sized breads if you prefer.

5. Place the dough on the heated griddle. Cook for about 5 minutes on this side, or until bubbles begin to rise up in the dough, and small brown spots appear on the underside. Turn the bread over and cook for 5-7 minutes more on the second side. Remove the bread from the griddle and brush with melted ghee. Repeat with the remainder of the bread dough.

6. Cut the naan into fourths or small triangles. Serve hot.

The Kitchen Goddess

Potato Knishes

Makes 8 knishes, 6-8 servings

Knishes are irresistible treats! They can stand on their own as a simple meal with a salad, or you can keep them in the fridge for an easy snack anytime.

Dough:

2 1/2 c. unbleached flour

1 t. salt

2 t. baking powder

3 T. melted butter or canola oil

1 1/4 c. warm water

Filling:

2 T. olive oil

1 medium onion, diced

3 medium potatoes, peeled, cubed, and boiled until soft

1/2 c. cottage cheese (optional)

1 1/2 t. salt

1/2 black pepper

1 egg, beaten with 1 t. water

1. In a medium mixing bowl, combine the flour, salt, and baking powder. Drizzle the melted butter over the flour mixture and stir until the butter forms pea-sized lumps in the flour. Add the warm water and stir until the dough sticks together.

2. Turn the dough out onto a floured board and knead for 5 minutes, until smooth.

3. In a medium skillet, heat the olive oil over medium heat. Sauté the onion for 3-5 minutes, until translucent. Remove from the heat.

4. In a medium mixing bowl, mash the potatoes with a masher. Stir in the cooked onions, cottage cheese, salt, and pepper.

5. On a floured board, roll out the dough into a large square, about 1/4 inch thick. Cut the square into 8 small squares, about 4 inches by 4 inches.

6. Place 3 T. of the potato filling in the center of each square. Fold up the edges of the squares, pinching them together along each of the four edges to create a pyramid shape.

7. Preheat the oven to 375. Place the knishes on an oiled cookie sheet. In a small bowl, beat the egg together with the water and brush the mixture over the knishes with a pastry brush.

8. Bake the knishes for 15-20 minutes, until golden brown. Serve hot or at room temperature.

Whole Grain Bagels

Makes 10-12 bagels

There's nothing like a fresh, homemade bagel! They are easier to make than you think, and lots of fun, too.

1 T. (1 packet) dry yeast

2 3/4 c. warm water

1/4 c. honey

1 c. whole wheat flour

4 c. unbleached enriched white flour

1 c. spelt flour

2 t. salt

1 egg, beaten with 1 t. water

Toppings: poppy seeds, sesame seeds, salt, finely chopped onion, caraway seeds

1. In a mixing bowl, combine the yeast, warm water, and honey and whisk together. Let stand for 10 minutes, until foamy on top.

2. Combine the yeast mixture, whole wheat flour, white flour, spelt flour, and salt in the mixing bowl. Using an electric mixer: with a dough hook attachment, mix on low speed for 3 minutes, then on medium speed for 3-5 minutes more, until the dough is smooth and smooth and elastic. By hand: turn the dough out onto a floured board and knead for 10 minutes by hand, until the dough is smooth and elastic.

3. Cover the dough with a dish towel and let rise in a warm place for about 45 minutes.

4. Preheat the oven to 425. On the stove, fill a large soup pot with water, add 1 T. salt, and bring to a boil.

5. From the dough mixture, form round balls about 3 inches in diameter, rolling the balls on the counter to create a sphere. Using your finger, poke a hole in the center of each ball and stretch the dough to slightly widen the hole. Let the bagels rise for 25-30 minutes.

6. Drop the bagels into the boiling water and boil for 2 minutes; turn over with a slotted spoon and boil for 2 minutes on the other side.

7. Transfer boiled bagels to an oiled cookie sheet. Brush with the egg wash and sprinkle with the toppings you prefer.

8. Bake the bagels for 25-35 minutes, until golden brown and crunchy on the outside. Cool and slice the bagels in half. Serve toasted.

The Kitchen Goddess

Parvati, the Embodiment of Creative Energy, in the main temple at Shoshoni Yoga Retreat.

Chocolate-Cinnamon Babke

Serves 10-12

This Eastern European coffee cake is updated here with Central American spices. The result is a spicy, sweet cake perfect for brunch or dessert. The cayenne pepper can be omitted for sensitive palates.

1 T. (1 packet) dry yeast

1/4 c. sugar or sucanat

3/4 c. warm water

1 c. milk or soymilk

3 T. canola oil or melted butter

1 egg, beaten

5 c. unbleached enriched flour

1/2 t. vanilla

1/2 t. salt

Filling:

2 c. semisweet chocolate chips

2 T. unsweetened cocoa

1/4 c. walnuts, chopped

1 medium apple, peeled and chopped

2 t. cinnamon

2 t. lemon juice

1 t. vanilla

1/2 t. salt

pinch cayenne pepper

4 T. butter, chopped

1. In a medium mixing bowl, combine the yeast, sugar, and warm water and whisk together. Let stand for 10 minutes, until foamy on top. Add the milk, canola oil, egg, flour, vanilla, and salt. Stir together until the dough starts to stick together. Turn the dough onto a floured work surface and knead for 5 minutes, until the dough is smooth.

2. Cover the dough with a dish towel, place in a warm place, and let rise for 45 minutes.

3. Place the chocolate chips in the mixing bowl of a food processor. Pulse 2 or 3 times to chop the chocolate. Add the cocoa, walnuts, apples, cinnamon, lemon juice, vanilla, salt, and cayenne. Pulse the food processor 3 or 4 more times to combine.

4. On a floured work surface, roll out the dough into a large oval, about 1/2 inch thick. Spread the filling mixture over the surface of the oval, leaving 1/2 inch with no filling around the sides. Sprinkle the butter over the surface of the filling.

5. Roll up the oval lengthwise into a log shape, pulling the dough towards you as you roll. Pinch the long end shut.

(cont. on next page)

Chocolate-Cinnamon Babke (Cont.)

6. Preheat the oven to 375. Oil and flour a Bundt pan or tube pan. Place the dough roll into the pan, seam down. Pinch the short ends together. Cover with a towel, place in a warm place, and let rise for 45 minutes.

7. Bake the babke for 35-45 minutes, until golden on top and hollow-sounding when thumped.

8. Remove from the oven, cool for 15-20 minutes, then turn the babke out upside-down onto a serving tray. Slice when cool into 10 or 12 slices.

Triple Berry Muffins

These muffins make a delightful breakfast or mid-afternoon snack. As with all muffins, they are best when eaten the same day they are baked.

2 c. unbleached enriched flour

2 1/2 t. baking powder

1/2 t. salt

2 eggs, beaten

1 c. milk or soymilk

1/3 c. sugar or sucanat

1/3 c. maple syrup

1/4 c. canola oil

1 t. vanilla

1/3 c. blueberries, fresh or frozen

1/3 c. raspberries, fresh or frozen

1/3 c. blackberries, fresh or frozen

1. Preheat the oven to 375. In a small mixing bowl, combine the flour, baking powder, and salt.

2. In a medium mixing bowl, beat the eggs together with the milk. Add the sugar, maple syrup, canola oil, and vanilla and beat until combined.

3. Fold the flour mixture into the wet ingredients, stirring 10-12 times, until the ingredients are just combined. The mixture will be slightly lumpy. Fold the berries into the batter.

4. Oil and flour a 12-cup muffin tin. Fill each muffin cup about 2/3 full. Bake the muffins for 15-20 minutes, until golden.

5. Remove from the oven, cool for 10 minutes, and loosen the muffins from the pan with a knife.

Molasses Rye Bread

Makes 2 loaves

Rye bread is comforting and homey, a heavier, denser bread. It is perfect for sandwiches and as an accompaniment to soups in the wintertime.

1 T. (one package) dry yeast

2 c. warm water

1/4 c. molasses

2 c. rye flour

4 c. unbleached enriched flour

2 t. salt

2 t. caraway seeds

1. In a mixing bowl, combine the yeast, warm water, and molasses and whisk together. Let stand for 10 minutes, until foamy.

2. Add the rye flour, unbleached flour, salt, and caraway seeds, and stir together. Using an electric mixer: Knead the dough using a dough hook attachment for 3 minutes on low speed, and 5 minutes on medium speed, until the dough is smooth and elastic. By hand: Turn the dough out onto a floured board and knead for 10 minutes, until the dough is smooth and elastic.

3. Place the dough in an oiled bowl, cover with a dish towel, and put in a warm place. Let rise for 1 hour.

4. Oil two 9-inch loaf pans. Punch down the dough and divide into two halves. Roll each half out into a 9-inch wide rectangle, then roll the dough into a loaf, pinching the seam shut. Place each loaf in a loaf pan, brush with oil, cover, and let rise for 1 hour.

5. Preheat the oven to 400. Bake the loaves for 45 minutes-1 hour, until deep golden and hollow-sounding when thumped. Remove from the oven and remove from the loaf pans immediately. Place loaves on a cooling rack and let cool completely before slicing.

Banana Pancakes

Serves 4

Delicious and easy, these pancakes are great for a special weekend breakfast! You can whisk the dry ingredients together the night before to save time in the morning.

3/4 c. whole wheat flour

3/4 c. unbleached enriched flour

1/4 c. sugar or sucanat

1 1/2 T. baking powder

1/2 t. salt

1 1/2 c. milk or soymilk

3 T. canola oil

2 eggs

1 t. vanilla

1 c. bananas, mashed

1. In a small bowl, combine the wheat flour, unbleached flour, sugar, baking powder and salt.

2. In another mixing bowl, whisk together the milk, canola oil, eggs, vanilla, and bananas. Fold the dry ingredients into the wet ones, mixing gently until just combined. Do not over mix; the batter will be lumpy.

3. Heat a griddle or cast-iron skillet over medium heat. Use 1 t. of canola oil to oil the skillet. Drop 1/4 c. of batter into the skillet. When the pancake looks dry on top and has bubbles throughout the surface, turn it over. Cook for 1 minute on the second side. Repeat for all pancakes.

4. Serve hot with maple syrup or fruit syrup.

The Kitchen Goddess

English Muffins

English muffins are so simple to make! They make a wonderful addition to any breakfast, and are also great for sandwiches and spreads.

1 T. (1 packet) dry yeast

1 c. warm water

2 T. honey

1/4 c. canola oil

1 1/2 c. whole wheat flour

1 1/2 c. unbleached enriched flour

1 t. salt

1/2 c. cornmeal

1. In a medium bowl, whisk together the yeast, warm water, and honey. Let stand for 10 minutes, until foamy.

2. Fold in the canola oil, wheat flour, unbleached flour, and salt. Mix until the dough starts to stick together. Using an electric mixer: With the dough hook on, mix the dough for 2 minutes on low speed and then 5 minutes on medium speed, until smooth and elastic. By hand: Turn the dough out onto a floured board and knead for 10 minutes, until smooth an elastic.

3. Place the dough in a bowl, cover, and put in a warm place. Let rise for 45 minutes.

4. Punch down the dough. Turn the dough onto a floured work surface and roll out to 1/2 inch thick. Using a 3-inch round cutter, cut circles out of the dough. Sprinkle the cornmeal on a cookie sheet and place the English muffins on the cornmeal. Dust more cornmeal on the top of the muffins. Cover with a dish towel and let rise for 15 minutes.

5. Heat a griddle or cast iron skillet over medium-low heat. Place 3 or 4 English muffins on the griddle at a time. Cook the muffins for 10 minutes on each side, until deep golden in color. Remove from the heat, let cool, and split with a fork. Repeat with the other muffins.

6. Toast the muffins before serving.

"Peacock with Fingers" by Faith Stone

"One evening, while I was staying with Rudi [Swami Rudrananda], he announced that we were all going out for Chinese food. Rudi took the whole lot of us, about 25 people, out to dinner in Chinatown. It was incredible food. The best I've ever tasted, still to this day. All the Chinese waiters knew Rudi. The owner came out to talk with him also. Rudi ordered everything. Huge platters of every kind of Chinese delight were passed around including steaming bowls of soup and noodles and tender puffed dumplings, sweet flavors, sour flavors, spicy and pungent. The restaurant took on a party atmosphere. Rudi laughed and joked with everyone. Anywhere he went was more special, brighter, and happier just because he was there. When Rudi was in a room, it was as though someone had turned up the lights. He lit up everything."

— **Sri Shambhavananda**

Condiments, Dressings, and Accompaniments

Baba Ganoush   133

Tofu Feta and Cashew Dip   134

Mixed Olive Tapenade   135

Creamy Cilantro Dressing   136

Creamy Sundried Tomato Dressing   137

Japanese Ginger Dressing   138

Sesame Goddess Dressing   139

Sweet and Sour Sauce   140

"Cheeseless" Sauce   141

Raita   142

Cranberry Chutney   143

Pear-Mint Chutney   144

Tofu Feta   145

Tofu Sour Cream   146

Homestyle Gravy   147

Jicama Pico de Gallo   148

Avocado Slaw   149

Baba Ganoush

Serves 4

Baba ganoush is a favorite spread at Shoshoni. Serve it with crackers, pita bread, or vegetable sticks.

1 medium eggplant, peeled and cubed into 1-inch cubes

1 t. salt

2 cloves garlic

1/4 c. olive oil

1/2 c. tahini

juice of 1 medium lemon

1. In a medium mixing bowl, sprinkle 1 t. of salt over the eggplant and toss to coat. Let sit for 20 minutes, until beads of moisture appear on the surface of the eggplant. Wipe the moisture off with a paper towel.

2. Preheat the oven to 400. In a medium glass baking dish, toss the eggplant, garlic, and olive oil. Cover the dish with foil, and bake covered for 20 minutes. Bake uncovered for another 10 minutes, until the eggplant is golden brown and very soft.

3. In a food processor, combine the roasted eggplant and garlic, tahini, and lemon juice. Puree the mixture until smooth. You may add more salt to taste.

Tofu Feta and Cashew Dip

Serves 4

This dip is full of protein and has a wonderful, creamy flavor! It is perfect served on crackers or garlic toast.

1/2 c. raw cashews

1/4 c. parsley

1/2 c. water

1 recipe Tofu Feta, p. 145

1 T. lemon juice

1 t. soy sauce or tamari

1/4 t. salt

1/2 t. garlic powder

1/2 t. paprika

dash cayenne pepper

1. In a blender, blend the cashews, parsley, and water together until almost smooth. The mixture may have a few small lumps. Transfer the mixture to a food processor.

2. Add the Tofu Feta, lemon juice, soy sauce, salt, garlic powder, paprika, and cayenne, and process until smooth.

3. Serve room temperature or refrigerated.

The Kitchen Goddess

Mixed Olive Tapenade

Serves 4-6

For olive lovers, there is no better way to enjoy bread than with this delicious olive spread. Try it tossed on pasta, too, for a special treat.

1 c. oil-cured black olives, pitted

1 c. green olives, pitted

1/4 c. kalamata olives, pitted

1 T. olive oil

2 t. lemon juice

1 t. rosemary

1/2 t. red chili flakes

1/4 t. grated lemon zest

1. In a food processor, combine all ingredients. Pulse 3-4 times, until the mixture looks finely chopped, but is not a paste. Serve room temperature or cold.

Creamy Cilantro Dressing

This salad dressing combines the tangy, fresh taste of cilantro with lime juice. Using silken tofu as the base, you'll never miss the dairy.

1 lb. firm silken tofu

1/2 c. olive oil

1/3 c. lime juice or lemon juice

1/4 c. honey

1/4 c. water

1 c. cilantro, coarsely chopped

1/2 medium cucumber, seeded and chopped

2 T. onion, finely chopped

1 t. garlic powder

2 t. salt

1/2 t. black pepper

1. In a blender, combine all ingredients. Pulse a few times to mix, then blend on medium speed for 1 minute, until smooth. Serve cold on salads or as a dip with vegetables.

Creamy Sundried Tomato Dressing

This salad dressing reminds me of an old favorite, Thousand Island dressing, without the dairy. It has a kick of Italian spices, too, that make it a favorite with Mediterranean meals.

1/2 c. sundried tomatoes

1 c. boiling water

1 lb. firm silken tofu

1/2 c. olive oil

1/3 c. cider vinegar

1/4 c. honey

1 T. soy sauce or tamari

1 T. Dijon mustard

1 T. onion, finely chopped

1 T. parsley, finely chopped

1 t. oregano

1 t. basil

2 t. salt

1/2 t. black pepper

1. In a small bowl, pour the boiling water over the sundried tomatoes. Let sit for 20 minutes, until the tomatoes absorb the water and soften.

2. In a blender, combine the silken tofu, tomatoes and their soaking water, olive oil, vinegar, honey, soy sauce, mustard, onion, parsley, oregano, basil, salt, and pepper. Pulse a few times to combine, then blend on medium speed for 1 minute, until smooth. Serve over green salad.

Japanese Ginger Dressing

Serves 6-8

This salad dressing is a favorite with green salads, and also with marinated vegetables. Its delicious secret is pickled ginger, available in specialty foods stores and some grocery stores.

1/2 c. canola oil

1/2 c. white miso

1/2 c. pickled ginger

1/3 c. rice vinegar

2 T. toasted sesame oil

1/4 c. honey

1 T. soy sauce

1/2 t. paprika

1/2 t. white pepper

1. In a blender, combine all ingredients. Puree on medium speed for 1- 2 minutes, until smooth.

The Kitchen Goddess

Sesame Goddess Dressing

Serves 6-8

This salad dressing has a tangy, nutty flavor. It goes well with Middle Eastern and Mediterranean meals.

1 c. olive oil

1/2 c. water

1/2 c. cider vinegar

1/2 c. tahini

1/3 c. honey

1/4 c. lemon juice

1/4 c. parsley, chopped

1 T. soy sauce

1 T. onion, chopped

1/2 t. garlic powder

1 t. oregano

2 t. salt

1/2 t. black pepper

1. In a blender, combine all ingredients. Puree on medium speed for 1-2 minutes, until smooth.

Sweet and Sour Sauce

Serves 6

 *Sweet and sour sauce has long been a staple of Asian cooking in the U.S. This healthy version is made with everyday ingredients. Try it as a dipping sauce for Cream Cheese Wontons, p. 27, or Chinese Dumplings with Cabbage and Star Anise, p. 28.*

1 c. cold vegetable stock or water

1/4 c. rice vinegar

1/4 c. honey

1 T. tomato paste

2 T. soy sauce

1 T. corn starch

1/2 t. ground ginger

1/4 t. garlic powder

1/2 t. salt

1. In a small saucepan, whisk all ingredients together. Place the saucepan on the stove over low heat.

2. Heat the sauce, whisking constantly, until it just begins to boil and thickens.

3. Remove from the heat and cool the sauce. Serve room temperature or cold.

"Cheeseless" Sauce

Serves 6-8

This sauce has consistently been one of the most popular items on the Shoshoni menu. Over and over, people request the recipe. Delicious on steamed vegetables, baked potatoes, and noodles, it has no dairy.

1/2 red pepper, stem and seeds removed

1/2 c. tahini

1/2 c. raw cashews

2 c. water or plain soymilk

1/2 c. olive oil

1/2 c. nutritional yeast flakes

1/4 c. soy sauce

1 T. lemon juice

1 t. salt

1/2 t. garlic powder

1/4 t. tumeric

1/4 t. paprika

pinch cayenne pepper

1. Over the stove flame, roast the red pepper for 3-5 minutes, until the skin begins to char. Let cool, then rub the skin off with your fingers.

2. In a blender, combine the red pepper with the rest of the ingredients. Blend for 1-2 minutes, until smooth. Transfer the sauce to a medium saucepan.

3. Over medium heat, heat the sauce, stirring frequently, until it just begins to boil and thicken. You may add more water if you prefer a thinner sauce. Remove from the heat and serve immediately.

Raita

This simple Indian condiment is part salad, part cool yogurt. Serve it with curry dishes to cool the heat of the spices!

1 c. plain yogurt

1 medium carrot, peeled and grated

1/2 medium cucumber, peeled, seeded, and grated

1 t. ground coriander

1/2 t. salt

1. Combine all ingredients in a small bowl and mix well. Serve cold.

Cranberry Chutney

Serves 4-6

Cranberries are a New World fruit, but their tangy flavor is the perfect partner for Indian dishes. Try this chutney with Tandoori Tempeh, p. 94.

2 c. dried cranberries

1 c. water

2 T. lemon juice

1/4 c. maple syrup

1 t. grated orange rind

1/2 t. cardamom

1 cinnamon stick

pinch cayenne pepper

1. In a medium saucepan, combine all ingredients. Bring to a boil over medium heat. Reduce heat and simmer for 5-7 minutes, until the cranberries are soft.

2. Take out the cinnamon stick. Transfer the chutney to a blender and pulse 3-4 times, until the mixture looks like applesauce, but is not totally smooth. Transfer the chutney to a medium bowl.

3. Cool the chutney. Serve room temperature or cold.

Condiments, Dressings, and Accompaniments

Pear-Mint Chutney

This cooling chutney is my all-time favorite. The astringent taste of the mint combines perfectly with the pears. Make it in summer, when the ingredients are abundant.

5 medium pears, peeled, seeded, and chopped

1/4 c. maple syrup

2 T. lemon juice

1/2 c. fresh mint, chopped

pinch salt

1. In a medium saucepan, combine the pears, maple syrup, and lemon juice. Bring to a boil over medium heat. Reduce heat, cover, and simmer for 5-7 minutes, until the pears soften.

2. Transfer pears to a food processor. Add mint and salt, and pulse 3-4 times to combine. The chutney should look like applesauce, chunky rather than smooth.

3. Cool the chutney. Serve room temperature or cold.

Tofu Feta

Serves 6-8

This recipe has appeared in all of the Shoshoni cookbooks – and for good reason! Tofu feta is versatile, easy, and a wonderful alternative to dairy.

1 lb. firm tofu

2 T. fresh lemon juice

1 T. minced chives

1 t. salt

1 t. garlic powder

1 T. minced fresh dill or 1 t. dried dill

1 t. olive oil

1. Combine half the tofu with all of the remaining ingredients in a food processor. Process for about 1 minute, until smooth.

2. In a small bowl, mash the remaining tofu with a fork and stir into the blended mixture. Refrigerate until ready to use.

Tofu Sour Cream

Serves 6-8

Silken tofu gives this recipe a smooth, creamy taste with no dairy and very little fat!

1 lb. silken tofu

1/2 t. salt

1 t. garlic powder

2 T. fresh lemon juice

1 t. rice vinegar

1. Place all ingredients in a food processor, and blend until smooth. Refrigerate until ready to serve.

Homestyle Gravy

Serves 6-8

Over the years at Shoshoni, I have observed that people often like the simplest dishes the best. Everyone wants the recipe for this gravy. It is wonderful on Mushroom Walnut Loaf, p. 103, or good old-fashioned mashed potatoes.

1/2 c. canola oil

1/2 c. unbleached enriched flour

1/2 c. onion, finely chopped

3 c. water

2 T. soy sauce

2 T. nutritional yeast flakes

1 t. garlic powder

1/2 t. thyme

1/2 t. rosemary

1/2 t. ground sage

1/4 t. black pepper

1. In a heavy-bottomed medium pot, whisk together the flour and oil until smooth. Heat the mixture over medium heat until it starts to bubble, whisking constantly. Turn the heat to medium-low.

2. Continue whisking the flour mixture over the heat until it starts to turn brown. When the mixture is a chocolate brown color, quickly stir in the onions, and whisk for 1 minute more.

3. Add the water, stirring constantly, and turn the heat down to low. Add the soy sauce, nutritional yeast flakes, garlic powder, thyme, rosemary, sage, and black pepper and stir to combine.

4. Heat the mixture on low, stirring frequently, until it just begins to boil. Remove from the heat and serve immediately.

Jicama Pico de Gallo

Serves 4-6

This Mexican condiment is so delicious, it could almost be a salad in itself! Serve it with Tostadas with Black Bean Refritos, p. 99.

3 medium tomatoes, seeded and diced

1/2 red onion, diced

1 tomatillo, seeded and diced

1 c. jicama, peeled and diced

1/2 c. cilantro, chopped

2 T. lemon juice

1 t. salt

1/2 t. garlic powder

1. In a medium bowl, combine all ingredients and mix well, Refrigerate until ready to serve. Serve room temperature or cold.

The Kitchen Goddess

Avocado Slaw

This delicious slaw has Caribbean flavors. It is wonderful paired with Jamaican Jerk Tofu, p. 89.

4 c. green cabbage, shredded

1 c. red cabbage, shredded

1 medium carrot, grated

1/2 red pepper, thinly sliced

3 avocados

2 T. olive oil

2 T. lime juice

2 T. orange juice

1 1/2 t. salt

1/4 t. allspice

1. In a medium bowl, combine the green cabbage, red cabbage, carrot, and red pepper. Cut one of the avocados into 1/2-inch cubes and add to the vegetables.

2. In a food processor, combine the other two avocados, olive oil, lime juice, orange juice, salt, and allspice. Puree until smooth.

3. Toss the dressing mixture over the vegetables and stir to coat. Refrigerate until ready to serve.

"Contremporary Vajra Yogini, Rainbow Body"
by Faith Stone

"We are jaded in our culture by the abundance of everything. We don't smell, taste or experience food anymore. Food becomes something that is just given to us on a plate. The scent of a flower, the scent of a butter lamp burning, the offering of rice, the taking of pure water, all these things are elements. They have a vibration that corresponds to a vibration inside of you. They can invoke finer, more basic types of energies within you."

– Sri Shambhavananda

Sweet Treats and Desserts

Ayurvedic Energy Balls   153

Vegan Chocolate Cake   154

Cheesecake Brownies   155

Simple Peanut Butter Cookies   156

Oatmeal Raisin Cookies   157

Hope's Apple Cake   158

Custard Fruit Tart   159

Apple Dumplings   160

Ginger Cookies   161

Chocolate Orange Mousse   162

Ayurvedic Energy Balls

These popular treats pack a punch with protein and whole grains for extra energy. They are also very easy to make and kids love them!

1 c. rolled oats

1/2 c. unsweetened flake coconut

1/4 c. sesame seeds

4 dates, finely chopped

1/4 c. raisins

3/4 c. unsweetened peanut butter

1/2 c. honey

1 t. vanilla

1/4 t. cinnamon

1. In a medium mixing bowl, combine the oats, coconut, sesame seeds, dates, and raisins.

2. In a small mixing bowl, whisk together the peanut butter, honey, vanilla, and cinnamon. Stir the dry ingredients together with the peanut butter mixture until combined.

3. Form the mixture into 1-inch balls. Store in an airtight container at room temperature.

Vegan Chocolate Cake

There is nothing as comforting as a simple chocolate cake. You can dress this one up with frosting, or simply sprinkle it with powdered sugar for a very satisfying dessert!

1 1/2 c. unbleached enriched flour

1 c. brown sugar or sucanat

1/3 c. unsweetened cocoa powder

1 t. baking soda

1/4 t. salt

1 c. cold water or soymilk

1/4 c. canola oil

1 T. white vinegar

2 t. vanilla

1 c. semi-sweet chocolate chips

1. Preheat oven to 375. In a medium mixing bowl, combine the flour, sugar, cocoa powder, baking soda, and salt and whisk together.

2. In a small bowl, combine the water, canola oil, vinegar, and vanilla. Stir the wet ingredients into the dry ones, stirring until just combined. Do not overmix. Fold in the chocolate chips.

3. Oil a 9-inch round cake pan. Pour the batter into the pan and bake for 25-30 minutes, until a toothpick inserted in the center comes out clean.

4. Remove from the oven and let cool completely before slicing.

Cheesecake Brownies

Serves 8-10

These decadent brownies are dressed up for a black tie affair with real cheesecake swirled into the batter. Serve solo or top with fresh berries and whipped cream for an extra special dessert.

Cheesecake batter:

1 1/2 lb. (3 8-oz. packages)
cream cheese, softened at room
temperature

1 c. sugar

1 t. vanilla extract

3 eggs

Brownie batter:

2 c. flour

3/4 t. baking soda

pinch salt

1c. semi-sweet chocolate chips

10 T. butter, softened

1 1/2 c. sugar

3 eggs

1 1/2 t. vanilla extract

1. Preheat oven to 375. Grease a 9 x 13 inch baking dish, bottom and sides, or line with parchment paper, and set aside.

2. Mix the cream cheese, sugar, and vanilla in the bowl of a food processor, or with a hand mixer. Add in the eggs one at a time until the batter is smooth and integrated. Cover and set aside in the refrigerator until the brownie batter is ready.

3. For the brownie batter, combine flour, baking soda, and salt in a bowl and set aside.

4. Melt the chocolate chips in a small pan over medium heat, stirring often with a wooden spoon or heat-safe spatula to prevent burning. Remove from the heat when the chocolate is smooth and creamy.

5. In a large mixing bowl, beat the butter and sugar until creamy and soft. Add eggs, vanilla, and melted chocolate and stir until well combined.

6. Mix the dry ingredients into the wet mixture. Whisk 1-2 minutes to mix well. Avoid over-beating.

7. Pour about half of the brownie batter in the bottom of the baking dish. Smooth it out to coat the bottom thoroughly. Pour all of the cheesecake batter onto the brownie layer in the pan. Drop spoonfuls of the remaining brownie batter onto the cheesecake batter to distribute evenly. Use a thin knife to score 4 lines through all layers of the batter.

8. Bake for 25-30 minutes, until a toothpick inserted in the center comes out clean. Let cool for 5-10 minutes before slicing.

Simple Peanut Butter Cookies

Makes 2 dozen

These vegan cookies come out of the oven soft, and are rich and chewy. Try adding chocolate chips for an extra treat! Spelt flour may be substituted for the wheat flour if you have wheat sensitivity.

1 1/2 c. all-purpose flour

1/2 t. baking soda

1 t. salt

1/2 c. canola or light olive oil

1 c. sugar or sucanat

1 large egg, or egg replacer

1 c. peanut butter

2 T. milk or soymilk

1/2 t. vinegar

1 t. vanilla

1. Preheat oven to 375 and oil a cookie sheet.

2. Combine flour, baking soda, and salt in one bowl. In another bowl, beat the oil and the sugar together. Add in the egg or egg replacer, peanut butter, milk, vinegar, and vanilla.

3. Add the flour mixture to the wet ingredients and stir until just combined.

4. Drop tablespoons of the cookie dough onto a cookie sheet 2-3 inches apart. Flatten with the bottom of a cup or a fork.

5. Bake 10-12 minutes until the edges just barely begin to brown. The cookies will be too soft to handle while hot. Let cool 5-10 minutes and remove from the cookie sheet.

Oatmeal Raisin Cookies

Makes 2 dozen

These vegan cookies are so sweet and wholesome. They are simple to make and lend themselves to creativity. Try chocolate chips, crystallized ginger chunks, or toasted nuts in place of the raisins for your own inspired cookies.

1 c. canola oil

1 c. brown sugar

1 c. sugar or sucanat

1 T. vanilla extract

1/2 c. soymilk

2 c. flour

1 t. baking powder

1 t. baking soda

1/2 t. salt

2 1/2 c. rolled oats

1/2 c. raisins

1. Preheat oven to 350. Grease a cookie sheet and set aside.

2. Combine the canola oil, brown sugar, sugar, vanilla, and soymilk in a mixing bowl and stir until smooth. In another bowl, stir the flour, baking powder, baking soda, and salt together.

3. Stir the dry ingredients into the wet mixture and stir to combine well. Fold in the oats and raisins.

4. Drop the cookie dough in tablespoonfuls onto the prepared cookie sheet. Space the cookies 2-3 inches apart.

5. Bake 12-15 minutes. For softer cookies, remove from the oven after 12 minutes when they still seem soft. They will cool and solidify into a chewy and delicious cookie!

Hope's Apple Cake

Serves 8-10

This cake is Bhavani's favorite! Part apple cobbler, part blondie, it has a dense, chewy texture.

2 1/2 c. flour

2 t. baking powder

1 t. salt

2 eggs

1 1/2 c. brown sugar or sucanat

1/2 c. canola oil

1 t. vanilla

3 medium apples, peeled and chopped into small pieces

1. Preheat oven to 375. In a small bowl, combine the flour, baking powder and salt and whisk to combine.

2. In a medium mixing bowl, beat the eggs together with the sugar, canola oil, vanilla, and chopped apples. Stir the flour mixture into the wet ingredients until just incorporated. The mixture will be thick.

4. Oil a 9x13-inch glass pan. Press the apple mixture into the pan with your hands. Bake the cake for 30-40 minutes, until golden on top. It should be soft but not wet in the center.

5. Let cool completely before cutting.

The Kitchen Goddess

Custard Fruit Tart

Serves 6-8

This delicious dessert uses whatever fruit is in season! Slice up the fruit and arrange it artistically on the tart for a beautiful treat.

Crust:

1 1/2 c. unbleached enriched flour

1/2 t. salt

1/4 c. canola oil

1/4 c. cold milk

Custard:

1/3 c. brown sugar or sucanat

2 T. cornstarch

pinch salt

1 c. cold milk or soymilk

2 egg yolks

1 T. butter

1 t. vanilla

Toppings:

3 c. seasonal fresh fruit, sliced thinly: berries, apples, pears, kiwis, or peaches (do not use citrus fruits)

1. Preheat the oven to 400. Oil a 9-inch tart pan or pie pan. In a small mixing bowl, combine the flour and salt. Stir in the canola oil. Drizzle the milk over the crust mixture, mixing until just combined. Press the crust into the bottom and sides of the tart pan. Bake for 10-15 minutes, until golden. Remove from the oven and let cool.

2. In a medium sauce pan, whisk together the brown sugar, cornstarch, and salt. Whisk in the milk and egg yolks, stirring well. Heat the mixture over medium heat, whisking constantly, until it just begins to boil and thickens.

3. Remove the custard from the heat and stir in the butter and vanilla. Pour the custard over the crust. Cool the tart in the refrigerator until very cold.

4. Top the tart with fresh fruit slices just before serving. Serve cold.

Apple Dumplings

These dumplings are easy to make and incredibly delicious! Serve them with whipped cream or vanilla ice cream for a wonderful finish to a meal.

Dough:

2 c. unbleached enriched flour

1/2 t. baking powder

1/2 t. salt

6 T. unsalted butter

3/4 c. cold milk or soymilk

Filling:

3 medium apples, peeled and sliced thinly

3 T. brown sugar or sucanat

1 t. cinnamon

1 t. lemon juice

Syrup:

1/2 c. unsalted butter

1/2 c. brown sugar or sucanat

1 t. vanilla

1 c. apple juice

2 t. lemon juice

1 t. cinnamon

1. In a medium bowl, whisk together the flour, baking powder, and salt. Cut the butter into the flour mixture using a pastry blender or two forks. The butter pieces should be about the size of peas. Drizzle the milk over the flour mixture, and stir to combine. Do not overmix.

2. In another bowl, combine the apples, brown sugar, cinnamon, and lemon juice. Let sit for 10 minutes.

3. Turn the dough out onto a floured work surface and knead 5-7 times, until the ingredients are just incorporated. Roll the dough out into a large square, 1/4 inch thick. Cut the dough into 9 square pieces, each about 3 inches by 3 inches.

4. Oil a 9x13 inch baking pan. Place several apple slices in the middle of each square, and roll up the square into a tube. Place the dumplings in a row in the baking pan, seams down.

5. Preheat the oven to 375. In a medium saucepan, melt the butter for the syrup. Add the brown sugar and vanilla, and stir to combine. Do not boil the mixture. Remove from the heat and pour over the dumplings in the pan.

6. In a cup, mix the apple juice and lemon juice together, then pour over the dumplings.

7. Sprinkle the cinnamon over the top of the dumplings. Bake for 30 minutes, until golden brown. The top of the dumplings will be crispy, and the bottom soft. Remove from the oven and spoon the extra sauce over the top of the hot dumplings. Serve warm with whipped cream or ice cream.

The Kitchen Goddess

Ginger Cookies

Makes 2 dozen

These ginger cookies are a sweet end to any meal. A gentle digestive aid, the ginger is warming to the body. They can be made chewy or crispy for a traditional ginger snap!

1 3/4 c. flour

3/4 t. baking powder

1/4 t. baking soda

1/2 t. salt

1 T. ground ginger

1 t. cinnamon

Pinch of ground cloves

1/3 c. melted butter or canola oil

3/4 c. brown sugar

2 T milk or soymilk

1 egg or egg replacer

1/4 c. molasses

1. Preheat oven to 350. Oil a cookie sheet and set aside.

2. Mix the flour, baking powder, baking soda, salt, ginger, cinnamon, and cloves and set aside.

3. In another bowl, whisk the butter and brown sugar together. Add the milk, egg, and molasses, and whisk to combine.

4. Add the dry ingredients to the wet mixture and stir until just combined.

5. Drop the dough by the tablespoon on the prepared cookie sheet. Space the cookies 2-3 inches apart.

6. Bake 12 minutes for chewy cookies, or 15 minutes for crunchy gingersnaps. Remove from the oven. Let cool 5 minutes before removing from the cookie sheet.

Chocolate Orange Mousse

Serves 6

This fluffy delight is an easy, delicious dessert!

1 c. semi-sweet chocolate chips

3 3/4 cups heavy cream

1 T. orange zest

1 t. vanilla extract

3/4 c. powered sugar, sifted

1 T. orange zest for topping

1. In a double boiler, melt the chocolate, 3/4 cup of the heavy cream, orange zest, and vanilla extract. Remove the mixture once melted and let it cool to room temperature.

2. Mix 3 cups of the heavy cream and the powered sugar in a large aluminum bowl. Using an electric beater, whip the cream until soft peaks form. Be careful not to over-whip the mixture.

3. Very gently, fold the chocolate mixture into the whipped cream.

4. Chill the mousse in the refrigerator for at least 30 minutes. Spoon the mixture into individual serving cups. Or, fill a large pastry bag with the mousse and pipe it into serving cups. Sprinkle a little bit of orange zest on top of each cup. Serve immediately or chill for up to 8 hours before serving.

The Kitchen Goddess

Tara, the Goddess of Wisdom and Compassion, in the Ma Shrine
at Shoshoni Yoga Retreat.

"If a cook at a restaurant is having a bad day, if he doesn't want to be there and he hates what he's doing, all that goes right into the food that he's cooking. The people that eat that food will pick up the cook's negative vibration. And they will think about coming back and go, "Hmm...think I'll go somewhere else." That's the magic and the mystery of it. The important thing is the consciousness with which you live your life. You don't have to go live in the forest. What is important is your state of mind when you are performing the actions of your life."

– Sri Shambhavananda

Menu Ideas

Here are some sample holiday or special occasion menus that we use at Shoshoni. Try them for any special dinner or holiday feast!

Mediterranean Creamy Tomato Soup, p.34

Tomato, Cucumber, and Feta Salad, p.47

Broccoli Strudel, p.98

Pita Bread, p.118

Mixed Olive Tapenade, p.135

Green Salad with Sesame Goddess Dressing, p.139

Ginger Cookies, p.161

Cream Cheese Wontons, p.27 with Sweet and Sour Sauce, p.140

Thai Coconut Ginger Soup, p.43

Sesame Soba Noodles, p.73

Spicy Asian Grilled Green Beans and Tofu, p. 95

Green Salad with Japanese Ginger Dressing, p.138

Sesame Brown Rice, p.65

Chocolate Orange Mousse, p.162

Mulligatawny, p.40

Black Sesame Yams, p.55

Tandoori Tempeh, p.94

Steamed Rice

Naan Bread, p.120

Raita, p.142

Cranberry Chutney, p.143

Vegan Chocolate Cake, p.154

Tamale Soup, p.33

Calabacitas, p.56

Tostadas with Black Bean Refritos, p.99

Tofu Sour Cream, p.146

Jicama Pico de Gallo, p.148

Steamed Quinoa

Apple Dumplings, p.160

Here is a week of menus for everyday cooking. They reflect what we might serve daily at Shoshoni. For a meal at home, you can try a whole menu, or just make two dishes that go together well for a simple dinner.

Monday

Breakfast
Triple Berry Muffins, p.126
Tahini Barley Cereal, p.78
Fresh fruit

Lunch
Creamy Carrot Ginger Soup, p.37
Asparagus Filo Spring Rolls, p.26
French Lentil Salad, p.76
Steamed Kale

Dinner
Tofu Tacos with Tartar Sauce, p.106
Avocado Slaw, p.149
Shredded Citrus-Vegetable Salad, p.59
Steamed Quinoa

Tuesday

Breakfast
Whole Grain Bagels, p.122
Kasha Varnishkes, p.66
Fresh fruit and yogurt

Lunch
Sundried Tomato Chili
with Textured Soy Protein, p.38
Calabacitas, p.56
3-Bean Salad, p.67
Green Salad

Dinner
Chana Masala, p.70
Sweet Potato Koftas, p.22
Poori Bread, p.119
Steamed vegetables

Wednesday

Breakfast
Chocolate-Cinnamon Babke, p.124
Fresh fruit and yogurt

Lunch
Panzanetta, p.48
Butternut Squash Lasagne, p.90
Green Salad with
Creamy Cilantro Dressing, p.136

Dinner
Stuffed Portabella Mushrooms, p.24
Spinach Salad
with Warm Miso Dressing, p.54
Ethiopian Lentil Soup, p.42
Fresh Bread

The Kitchen Goddess

Thursday

Breakfast
Sweet Potato Spice Bread, p.115
Lakshman's Butternut Squash
and Coconut Kitchari, p.41
Fresh fruit

Lunch
Chinese Dumplings
with Cabbage and Star Anise, p.28
Sesame Asparagus Salad, p.49
Whole Wheat Noodles
with Asian Black Bean Sauce, p.102
Steamed rice

Dinner
Matzo Ball Soup, p.31
Almond Green Beans, p.51
Wild Rice and Celery Root Casserole, p.63
Simple Peanut Butter Cookies, p.156

Saturday

Breakfast
Banana Pancakes, p.128
Summer Fruit Muesli, p.80
Fresh fruit

Lunch
Grilled Corn Chowder
with Chipotle Peppers, p.36
Gorditas with Homestyle Pinto Beans, p.96
Jicama Pico de Gallo, p.148
Green Salad

Dinner
Jamaican Jerk Tofu, p.89
Coconut Bread, p.116
Rice and Peas
Avocado Slaw, p.149
Steamed Vegetables
Hope's Apple Cake, p.158

Friday

Breakfast
Potato Pancakes
with Homemade Applesauce, p.57
Coconut Cream of Wheat, p.79
Fresh fruit

Lunch
Thai Coconut-Ginger Soup, p.43
Pad Thai Style Vegetable Curry, p.105
Jasmine Fried Rice with Pineapple, p.64

Dinner
Baba Ganoush, p.133
Summer Vegetable Pie, p.104
Fattouch Salad, p.53
Fresh bread
Custard Fruit Tart, p.159

Sunday

Breakfast
English Muffins, p.129
Tempeh Skillet, p.77
Fresh fruit

Lunch
Idli Sambar, p.39
Indian Style Mashed Potatoes, p.58
Curry Kidney Beans
with Homemade Cheese, p.68
Basmati Rice
Steamed Kale
Ginger Cookies, p.161

Dinner
Angel Hair Pasta
with Italian Salsa Fresca, p.91
Marinated Broccoli
and Summer Squash Salad, p.50
Green Salad with
Creamy Sundried Tomato Dressing, p.137

Menu Ideas

References

Muktananda, Swami. *Bhaguvan Nityananda of Ganeshpuri*. South Fallsburg, NY: SYDA Foundation, 1996.

Muktananda, Swami. *Mystery of the Mind*. South Fallsburg, NY: SYDA Foundation, 1981.

Muktananda, Swami. *Where Are You Going?* South Fallsburg, NY: SYDA Foundation, 1981.

Shambhavananda, Swami. *Spontaneous Recognition*. Eldorado Springs, CO: SGRY, 1995.

Shambhavananda, Sri. *A Seat By the Fire*. Rollinsville, CO: Prakasha Press, 2005.

Stone, Faith. *Rudi and the Green Apple*. Rollinsville, CO: SGRY, 2000.

A double rainbow over the Meditation Temple at Shoshoni Yoga Retreat

Index

A

adzuki beans
  Three Bean Salad 67
  Gingered Adzuki Beans 71
Almond Green Beans 51
almonds
  Spinach Salad with Warm Miso Dressing 54
  Summer Fruit Muesli 80
Angel Hair Pasta with Italian Salsa Fresca 91
Apple Dumplings 160
apples
  Curry Apple Squash Soup 32
  Potato Pancakes with Homemade Applesauce 57
  Summer Fruit Muesli 80
  Chocolate-Cinnamon Babke 124
  Custard Fruit Tart 159
asafetida xiv, 23
asparagus 49
Asparagus Filo Spring Rolls 26
Avocado Slaw 149
Ayurvedic Energy Balls 153

B

Baba Ganoush 133
Babaji iii, ix
Bagels, Whole Grain 122
Banana Pancakes 128
bananas 80
barley 78
basil
  Bruschetta 21
  Lima Bean and Soy "Sausage" Soup 35
  Panzanetta 48
  Polenta Squares with Eggplant Relish 75
  Butternut Squash Lasagne 90
  Angel Hair Pasta with Italian Salsa Fresca 91
  Tofu Parmesan with Carrot Marinara Sauce 110-111
  Creamy Sundried Tomato Dressing 137
Black Bean Sauce 102
blackberries 126

Black Sesame Yams 55
blueberries 126
broccoli 50
Broccoli Strudel 98
Brownies, Cheesecake 155
Butternut Squash Lasagne 90

C

cabbage
  Chinese Dumplings with Cabbage and Star Anise 28
  Shredded Citrus-Vegetable Salad 59
  Tofu Tacos with Vegan Tartar Sauce 106
  Avocado Slaw 149
Calabacitas 56
cardamom
  Indian-Style Mashed Potatoes 58
  Chana Masala 70 v
  Tofu Tikka Masala 92
  Cranberry Chutney 143
carrots
  Asparagus Filo Spring Rolls 26,
  Matzo Ball Soup 31
  Mulligatawny Soup 40
  Thai Coconut-Ginger Soup 43
  Tofu Parmesan with Carrot Marinara Sauce 110-111
Carrot-Ginger Soup, Creamy 37
cashews
  Curry Kidney Beans with Homemade Cheese 68
  Tofu Feta and Cashew Dip 134
cauliflower
  Vegetable Bhajis 23
  Pad Thai Style Vegetable Curry 105
Chana Masala 70
Cheesecake Brownies 155
Chocolate-Cinnamon Babke 124
Chocolate Orange Mousse 162
chutnies
  Cranberry Chutney 143
  Pear-Mint Chutney 144
Cilantro Dressing, Creamy 136
cinnamon 161

coconut
    Lakshman's Butternut Squash and Coconut
        Kitchari 41
    Thai Coconut-Ginger Soup 43
    Jamaican Jerk Tofu 89
    Ayurvedic Energy Balls 153
Coconut Bread 116
Coconut Cream of Wheat 79
collard greens 52
cookies
    Simple Peanut Butter Cookies 156
    Oatmeal Raisin Cookies 157
    Ginger Cookies 161
Corn Chowder, Grilled 36
cottage cheese
    Mushroom-Walnut Loaf 103
    Potato Knishes 121
Cranberry Chutney 143
Cream Cheese Wontons 27
cucumber
    Tomato, Cucumber, and Feta Salad 47
    Creamy Cilantro Dressing 136
    Raita 142
Cucumber Rice Noodle Salad 74
Curry Apple Squash Soup 32
Curry Kidney Beans with Homemade Cheese 68
Custard Fruit Tart 159

D

dates 153
Divine Mother x
Durga x, xiii

E

eggplant
    Polenta Squares with Eggplant Relish 75
    Baba Ganoush 133
Eggplant Curry, Roasted 93
eggs
    Matzo Ball Soup 31
    Mushroom-Walnut Loaf 103
    Sweet Potato Spice Bread 115
    Triple Berry Muffins 126
    Banana Pancakes 128
    Cheesecake Brownies 155

Hope's Apple Cake 158
English Muffins 129
Ethiopian Lentil Stew - Yemesir Wat 42

F

Fattouch Salad 53
fenugreek 93
feta
    Stuffed Portabella Mushrooms 24
    Tomato, Cucumber, and Feta Salad 47
    Calabacitas 56
    Curry Kidney Beans with Homemade Cheese 68
    Tofu Feta 145
filo
    Asparagus Filo Spring Rolls 26
    Summer Vegetable Pie 104

G

ginger xvii
    Creamy Carrot-Ginger Soup 37
    Thai Coconut-Ginger Soup 43
    Sesame Soba Noodles 73
    Whole Wheat Noodles with Asian Black Bean
        Sauce 102
    Pad Thai Style Vegetable Curry 105
    Sweet Potato Spice Bread 115
    Japanese Ginger Dressing 138
Ginger Cookies 161
Gingered Adzuki Beans 71
goat cheese 24
green beans
    Almond Green Beans 51
    Three-Bean Salad 67
    Spicy Asian Grilled Green Beans and Tofu 95
Grilled Corn Chowder 36

H

hing xiv
Homemade Applesauce 57

I

Idli Sambar 39

Indian-Style Mashed Potatoes 58

The Kitchen Goddess

J

Jamaican Jerk Tofu 89
Jasmine Fried Rice with 64
Jicama Pico de Gallo 148

K

Kali xi, xiii
Kasha Varnishkes 66

L

Lakshmi x, xiii, 60
lentils
    Idli Sambar 39
    Mulligatawny Soup 40
Lentil Stew, Ethiopian - Yemesir Wat 42
Lentil Salad, French 76
lettuce
    Fattouch Salad 53
    Tostadas with Balck Bean Refritos 99
    TVP Tacos 109
Lima Bean and Soy "Sausage" Soup 35

M

mantra xii
Maple-Walnut Quick Bread 117
Ma Shrine xi, 72, 163
Matzo Ball Soup 31
miso
    Sesame Asparagus Salad 49
    Three-Bean Salad 67
    Whole Wheat Noodles with Asian Black Bean
        Sauce 102
Miso Dressing 54
Mixed Olive Tapenade 135
Molasses Rye Bread 127
Mulligatawny Soup 40
Mushroom-Walnut Loaf 103
Mushrooms, Stuffed Portabella 24

N

Naan Bread 120
nutritional yeast xvi, 147

O

Oatmeal Raisin Cookies 157
oats
    Summer Fruit Muesli 80
    Ayurvedic Energy Balls 153
orange zest 162

P

Pad Thai Style Vegetable Curry 105
Panzanetta 48
peanut butter 156
Pear-Mint Chutney 144
pears 159
peas
    Ethiopian Lentil Stew - Yemesir Wat 42
    Jasmine Fried Rice with Pineapple 64
    Jamaican Jerk Tofu 89
pineapple 64
Pita Bread 118
Polenta Squares with Eggplant Relish 75
Poori Bread 119
Potato Knishes 121
Potato Pancakes with Homemade Applesauce 57

R

raisins
    Ayurvedic Energy Balls 153
    Oatmeal Raisin Cookies 157
Raita 142
raspberries 126
ricotta cheese
    Butternut Squash Lasagne 90
    Broccoli Strudel 98
Roasted Eggplant Curry 93
rye 127

S

Salsa Fresca 91
Saraswati x, xiii, 72
Sesame Brown Rice 65
Sesame Goddess Dressing 139
Sesame Soba Noodles 73
Shredded Citrus-Vegetable Salad 59
soba noodles 73

Index

soymilk 160
soy "sausage" 35
spaghetti 102
spelt
  Summer Fruit Muesli 80
  Whole Grain Bagels 122
Spicy Asian Grilled Green Beans 95
Spinach Salad with Warm Miso Dressing 54
Summer Vegetable Pie 104
Sundried Tomato Chili 38
Sweet and Sour Sauce 140
Sweet Potato Koftas 22
Sweet Potato Spice Bread 115

T

tahini 141
Tahini Barley Cereal 78
Tamale Soup 33
Tempeh Skillet 77
Tempeh, Tandoori 94
Three-Bean Salad 67
Tofu Feta 145
Tofu Feta and Cashew Dip 134
Tofu Meatballs 20
Tofu Sour Cream 146
Tofu Tikka Masala 92
Triple Berry Muffins 126
tumeric 22
TVP Tacos 109

V

vanilla 160
Vegetable Bhajis 23

W

walnuts 25
Whole Wheat Noodles with Asian 102
Wild Rice and Celery Root 63

Y

yams 58
Yemesir Wat 42
yogurt 142

The Kitchen Goddess

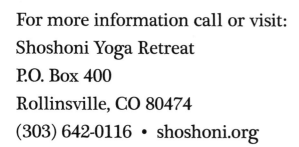

also available from
Shoshoni Yoga Retreat

The Shoshoni Cookbook
Anne Saks and Faith Stone

Yoga Kitchen
Faith Stone and Rachael Guidry

Rudi and the Green Apple
Faith Stone

Spontaneous Recognition
Sri Shambhavananda

A Seat by the Fire
Sri Shambhavananda

Sacred Journey
Swami Kripananda

Purchase these titles from your local bookstore or directly from:

Shoshoni Yoga Retreat
P.O. Box 400
Rollinsville, CO 80474
(303) 642-0116

also available online at:
shoshoni.org

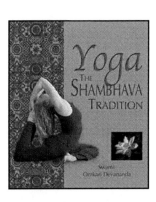

Yoga in the Shambhava Tradition
Swami Omkari Devananda